"When a partner dies, we begin a long journey down a path we'd rather not take, and we may imagine that life could never be bearable again. The poems in this 'handbook' offer much more than guidance or comfort. Their searing honesty and vivid depictions of resilience offer us invaluable reassurance that our grieving, however painful, will not destroy our capacity to live with meaning—and even joy."

—JUDY NORSIGIAN

Executive Director of *Our Bodies, Ourselves*
and cofounder, Boston Women's Health Collective

"I wish this collection had been available when I was a new widow. What a spectacular group of women this is! If they were my circle of friends or therapy group, I would have gone to every meeting. Their reactions and experiences as widows are varied, but each woman brings her own special intelligence to mourning, managing alone, and making a new life. Poetry makes those experiences immediately, emotionally accessible."

—JACQUELINE M. S. WINTERKORN

M.D., Ph.D., Clinical Professor of Ophthalmology; Clinical Professor of
Ophthalmology in Neurology and Neuroscience at Weill Cornell Medical
College; Attending Ophthalmologist, NewYork-Presbyterian Hospital

"*The Widows' Handbook* is a powerful emotional guide for the bereaved, organized by the evolving experiences of 87 women. But it's also far more—a testament to the redemptive power of poetry even in the darkest hours of life, offering proof that when we put love and art together, life can face death on equal—or better—terms."

—DANIEL MENAKER

former Executive Editor-in-Chief at Random House Publishing Group, former
fiction editor at *The New Yorker,* and author of *A Good Talk* and *My Mistake*

"A beautiful collection of poetry written by women experiencing one of the most traumatic events in their lives. There is something in this book for every widow, regardless of where she is in her loss, from early in bereavement through the process of rebuilding. Truly an excellent resource that readers can go back to over and over again for support and guidance."

—ELLEN KAMP

President and cofounder, The W Connection:
Widows Helping Widows Rebuild Their Lives

The Widows' Handbook

Literature and Medicine

MICHAEL BLACKIE, EDITOR

CAROL DONLEY AND MARTIN KOHN, FOUNDING EDITORS

The Widows' Handbook

~

Poetic Reflections on Grief and Survival

~

Edited by Jacqueline Lapidus and Lise Menn

~

Foreword by Ruth Bader Ginsburg

~

The Kent State University Press

KENT, OHIO

Library of Congress Catalog Card Number 2013031960

ISBN 978-1-60635-204-5

Manufactured in the United States of America

LIBRARY OF CONGRESS CATALOGING-IN-PUBLICATION DATA

The Widows' Handbook : Poetic Reflections on Grief and Survival / edited by Jacqueline Lapidus and Lise Menn ; foreword by Ruth Bader Ginsburg.

pages cm. —

ISBN 978-1-60635-204-5 (softcover) ∞

1. American poetry—Women authors. 2. Loss (Psychology).
3. Grief—Poetry. 4. Widows' writings. I. Lapidus, Jacqueline, editor of compilation.
II. Menn, Lise, editor of compilation.

PS589.W48 2014

811.008'09287—dc23

2013031960

18 17 16 15 14   5 4 3 2 1

Contents

PART III: COPING (MORE OR LESS)

PART IV: A DIFFERENT LIFE

EPILOGUE

Foreword

Death of one's life partner is a loss like no other. Many who have suffered the loss have no words to convey their grief, their doubts about their ability to carry on alone, and their hopes for a future strengthened by the love that caused them to appreciate their own worth. Mainly through poetry, the compilers of this anthology have provided the words widows feel but often cannot speak. Fittingly, *The Widows' Handbook* is both empathetic and encouraging. The poems speak first of the long days and nights consumed by mourning, then of the need to tackle the necessities of living without the support that once sustained them, and ultimately of the capacity still to seek the joys of being alive.

Readers of *The Widows' Handbook* will return to favorite expressions that capture their own experiences as they indulge in remembrances, yet grow in their determination to survive, just as the one who loved them would have willed. I commend Jacqueline Lapidus and Lise Menn for an undertaking of extraordinary value to people coping with the strains and stress of widowhood and striving to make their independent work and days satisfying.

RUTH BADER GINSBURG
Associate Justice
Supreme Court of the United States

Introduction

We are proud to present the first anthology ever of poems by widows: women old and young, legally married or not, straight or gay, whose partners or spouses have died. The title of this book is only partly ironic: few songs, stories, or legends show us how to behave and survive as contemporary widows, our status often diminished as single women in a coupled society. How do you live with the absence of a love that has filled your life, the loss of the identity that being needed gave you? How do you bear it? Becoming a widow is likely to be the most painfully overwhelming change that most women ever face. Are there any choices? Is there a way to do it right? How can we do it at all?

These poems and essays express the ways that more than eighty women of our time have mourned, despaired, remembered, struggled, and perhaps reached places of peace or renewal. Many of these works are beautiful, but some, though eloquent, are not pretty. We chose them because we felt that they told the truth from and about the writer's heart, either directly or allusively, and because they told that truth in a way that felt like poetry. Although the prose pieces included here are not formatted as poems, we found them to be as transformative as poetry in their imagery, rhythm and feeling.

Some notable writers have published memoirs or poems about their first year or two of widowhood, but no collection has ever covered such a wide range of widows' experiences. This book is by and for widows, and also for our families and other people who want to understand us, who may be even more confused than we are about how being a widow feels and what has happened to our lives. While we chose to limit the contributors to women who had lost husbands and lovers, we hope that men whose partners have died will also find their feelings and some of their situations here.

The Widows' Handbook includes writing about mourning and its rituals, other people's responses to grieving widows, coping strategies and spiritual resources that help some of us, supportive people in our lives (or the lack of them), and how life goes forward: isolation, work, friends, dating, and sometimes even a new love or focus. It celebrates the resources that we draw on to attend to work, children, grandchildren, home, garden and, especially, to ourselves, once the first flurry of tasks is over and shock has turned to the realization that nothing will ever be the same. Only poetry can speak such difficult truths and convey feelings in images that incite readers to empathize so intensely. There is no psychobabble here, no "stages of grief," no preaching, no easy answers; no assumption that we are all alike or have the same beliefs, and no hypocrisy.

Our contributors come from, and live, all over the United States—and one in England. Some have written all their lives, some are published widely, some have won major prizes for poetry. Others started writing more recently, and for some, this is their first publication. The anthology grew out of our own connection: widowed college classmates reading each other's poems and realizing we had the elements of a book. As we made our selections from among nearly five hundred submissions and from poems that spoke to us in published collections, our conversations—with each other and with many of the authors who sent us their work—generated a sense of the solidarity, encouragement, and sustenance that helps all of us carry our grief and live our new lives in spite of our partners' irrevocable absence.

Many of the women whose work you are about to read told us they wished they had had a book like this to give them a few clues when they first became widows. Among the hundreds of different moods reflected here, you may find a match for your own as it fluctuates by the minute, the hour, the year. We hope you may find, somewhere in this collection, the small but real comfort of realizing that others have endured the same screaming pain and numbing solitude as you did. If you do not, these poems and essays may help you find the words you need to tell your own varieties of truth.

JACQUELINE LAPIDUS & LISE MENN

Widows

JACQUELINE LAPIDUS

You are the salt of the earth
If the salt has lost its savor, wherewith
shall it be salted?
　　—MATTHEW 5:13

She was driving home on a Friday night
suddenly he slumped forward in the passenger seat
and in mid-sentence he was gone *I pulled over,*
I called 911, I begged him, talk to me, talk to me!
Every move is sad and hard to make
the only positive distraction for her is work
her friends make sure she's not alone during the week,
rattling around in that enormous house *I'm numb,*
I'm on automatic pilot, I still can't talk

He was closing the summer house and didn't want help
The fridge was full of food for Thanksgiving
her pie was cooling on the rack any minute his key
would be turning in the lock
I called the caretaker and told him to look
everywhere, even up in the attic
He was in the kitchen, he'd had a stroke

He couldn't come to reunion, he was much too sick to travel
his students came to visit from around the world
the hospice people took wonderful care
the children were there at the very end
I was with him that day from the moment he opened his eyes
to the moment death closed them
no matter how prepared you are
you're never ready

Imagine your best friend the father of your children
arm clasped around your shoulders protecting
you from harm imagine the great love
of your life your perfect chef your audience
weak and wasted
hand reaching beyond but not really holding on
Imagine having everything that mattered
imagine it gone

She sits in the front pew, frail and dignified
under her black hat surrounded by relatives neighbors strangers
She takes the shovel in her shaking hands and throws earth
into the grave   she takes the ashes from the box
and casts them into the ocean
she lets waves of talk wash over her at the shiva
She eats everything chocolate she can get her hands on
she has no appetite she can't keep anything down

She remembers how beautiful he was
in his forties, with his wasp waist
and washboard chest she remembers
picking bits of blue lint out of his perfect navel
she remembers the velvet tip of his penis
the sounds he made and the tenderness
afterward, curled around her before falling asleep
even in his last years they didn't stop

She still subscribes, but her symphony seats
have been changed to the keyboard side:
I couldn't bear to see all those people
who remembered me with Tom Once
over dinner I told her, of course he loved you!
how could you doubt it?
and she burst into tears, *But he died!*

She's living the hermit life, surrounded by
memorials and thinking in half an hour he'll be
home, pull into the driveway, call at the usual time
She hasn't touched her room she's left it like a shrine
I am standing still while a tornado is ripping through my body

She's in the market buying tomatoes, she's
in a meeting about sewer districts, she sees him lying
on the hospital gurney, she sees
his golf clubs leaning against the wall
and falls on her knees

Grief takes sadness to new heights and throws it off the cliff.
Grief is as big and as whole as love,
it is a new tenant in your heart with a long lease
Every move is sad and hard to manage
Getting out of bed in the morning is a tremendous effort
I weep uncontrollably only to myself,
when I speak to him it's in the present tense
painful as it is, I now prefer loneliness to chatter
After he died, I became invisible.

I hate this! meaning the single room,
the oxygen tank the potty chair
the blowsy social worker in a nylon smock
with untweezed chin and flyaway hair,
and all those meals alone—*I hate this!*
I want to be with Don

Don't say he had a full life what a mercy he didn't suffer longer
don't tell us our memories will comfort us
don't insist we'll get over it and move on and meet someone.
Our grief mirrors our love.
Tell a widow that what she is going through
strikes terror into your heart.
Tell a widow you have much to learn from her when she's ready

Sometimes my grief overwhelms me. Last week
it occurred to me that I couldn't go back to my husband
or to the past Then, when I'm feeling better,
missing him so badly is actually reassuring—
how could I move on without feeling his impact on my life?

She's sitting at home instead of going out by herself
she's at their cabin every weekend with the grandchildren
she's obsessed with her research, staying all night in the lab

she's making soft sculptures bigger than life-size
She has given up looking for a job,
she says work doesn't matter, it has to be worthwhile
and come to her, and she must be the right person to do it
She says, *if I don't want to do something nobody can make me*
She dyes her hair a color not found in nature
she says next year she's going to retire
She says, after all the time she spent taking care of him
she deserves a rest. She too may die.
And then again, maybe not

Author's Note:
Grateful acknowledgment and loving thanks to all the women whose words and experiences inspired and contributed to this poem along with mine: Christine, Cynthia, Genevieve, Harriet, Jacquie, Judy, Laura, Lee, Margaret, Martha, Natalie, Paula and Sheila.

I
Bereft, Mourning

Cross-Country Lines

JANE HAYMAN

You are leaving
changing into leaf

breath
slipping away   in pale fires.

I barely hear you.   The sheets
are louder than
your voice

—they flutter above you,
unfolding

like leaves in a book
falling from a shelf.

It is your self
falling,   your self.

I wish I could
play with the wires
and put back the sound

that song
you sing in my sleep

Afterword

JANE HAYMAN

Last night I dreamed it all
in clear colors:
our house of weathered stone;
the sky, the river
blue and green as glass;
some lemon-colored mountains to the left
and, to the right, the rows
of golden lemon trees;
me in a long white dress, forever bridal
and you beside me, laughing,
your leopard face alive
(alive) in the lucid air.

Today the papers advertise your death.
The heart has failed
as it had failed so many times,
your heart, my heart.
Gone now, gone—
and gone that many-colored,
that elegant invention,
our unlived life.

Vigil

PATRICIA WELLINGHAM-JONES

The hospice nurse whispers
in your abandoned ear,
It's all right to go,
Pat will be OK.

The cats hold their silent vigil.
Java hunches against your thigh,
Smudge crouches on your lap,
both watch my every move
without a twitch.

I pull up your desk chair, stretch
my arm between bed rails,
hold your frail flaccid hand,
gently stroke.

The afternoon sun
travels its course in the sky,
windows grow dim.

Just before full dark
the cats leap from your bed,
dash outside, disappear.

Your eyes flare open in a wild stare.
You gasp, take two spaced breaths.
Eyelids at half mast, you leave
on an exhalation.

Head bowed I sit,
your warm hand in mine,
and wait.

Minutes later, with a long sigh
I rise, close your eyes.
Press my lips to your forehead,
pick up the phone.

The cats don't come back
until the next day.

Falling

MAUREEN TOLMAN FLANNERY

Coyote, wily as time, is used to pursuing
his swift nemesis off the edge of a cliff,
blurred legs spinning like wheels,
the momentum of chase propelling him

straight out over the canyon where his
being oblivious carries him, keeps him aloft.
Only when some vague sense of disequilibrium
suggest he check his ground does the looking down

send him plummeting through the nothing solid
where he is surprised to find himself.
For you the phone's ring was the movement
forward—off the edge of the world,

that trajectory from which it almost seems
you should be able to reverse the propeller
of numb limbs spinning, flailing,
that they might carry you back to the rim

of something firm that would hold your weight.
But you were racing onto air and have looked down.
Now you are free falling
and cannot see the bottom.

Threshold

ANN SINCLAIR

The not-yet widow stands at the closet door,
Surveys the shirts suspended in dark air,
The shoes arranged in neat pairs on the floor.

Decisions must be made. From what he wore
Select the things his body and mind can bear.
The not-yet widow stands at the closet door.

His presence fills the space. Her memories soar
Though his are gone. She wishes he were here
To rearrange the shoes on the closet floor.

He's not. One must decide. One can't restore.
To give to charity is to declare.
The not-yet widow stands at the closet door.

This shirt with snaps, well washed, will suit him more,
These woolen slippers, familiar, soft with wear.
No more those well worn boots on the closet floor.

Who makes pronouncements? Who assumes the chore
Of stating what he comprehends or cares?
The not-yet widow stands at the closet door,
Surveys the shoes in neat pairs on the floor.

Ironing at Dawn

COOPER GALLEGOS

You stand here ironing before dawn
the long-sleeved white shirt
you make stiff with starch
stepping on the arm as it trails the floor

He didn't come home last night
You expect the worst
certain the only thing
to keep him away
would be death
You imagine the funeral,
handing the fresh shirt to the mortician
Walking with grace like Jackie Kennedy
to view the body that looks back at you
with contempt buried beneath the full beard
His name in plastic letters on a sign at the door
like he always expected
Like a book signing

Ironing beneath the kitchen light at dawn
The first sense of widowhood hanging
comfortably like a shawl over
your shoulders

Your baby in his seat on the kitchen table,
an echo of his father
Grinning, leaving a trail of digested
milk that spills from one corner
of his lopsided mouth

Watching the path of the iron
back and forth
the white shirt taking shape
like he's come home to claim it.

Widow Mother

LUCIA MAY

I was sure there had been a crime and cover-up.
I was nine months pregnant
standing in a hospital corridor,
but not to have the baby.
A doctor told me that my husband was dead.

I thought to bargain with God
but I had an ultrasound photo
and she, kicking in my ribs,
had a name.

A nurse said, *"When you're thrown
in the water you have no
choice but to swim."*
To me at 23 it sounded profound
even without music and lighting,
but I still smelled him on my hands.

I bought a pack of cigarettes,
went home and waited
ten days for labor.

I pretended that her birth trumped him
while I traced his lips and ears on her,
as she bit my engorged breast.

The shower steamed and pounded
when my milk let down,
a spray of hot tears
mixing with new blood.

I Love the Vet

RUTH S. ROTHSTEIN

I love the vet who
takes care of my cats.
She has a direct line in.

She helped my beloved Coda
cross over to the other side.
"She was ready," the vet said.
"I know because she didn't fight me."

I helped Jacques
cross over to the other side.
He was ready.

Cemetery Haiku

RUTH S. ROTHSTEIN

If I could, I would
crawl in under the dirt and
cuddle up with you.

Is He Saved?

CAROLYN STEPHENS

The night Jeff lay dying, the overnight CNA asked me if my husband was saved. Saved? Out of context, I had no idea what she was asking me. Is this some medical term I should know? Organ donation? Wh—OH! I stupidly, finally, stammered, you mean, like, in Jesus?

Yes, she patiently replied. Is he saved?

Another day, I might have taken offense or refused to answer such a personal question coming from, essentially, an employee, someone whom we had known for only a week. But that night, all layers of social fabric between us were stripped away and we were just two people caring for my husband, who was clearly, quietly, failing in the room next door.

Saved? She was asking as a Christian, plainly concerned with the repose of Jeff's soul for all eternity.
I answered from the heart and without planning what to say.

We are spiritual people, I said.
We believe there are powers in this world we don't understand. We believe the world is made of energy that may change but does not dissipate. We believe in kindness and trying to do no harm as we go through life. But since you are asking me this question, I am sure that our beliefs are different from yours.
To answer what I think you are asking:
He is not afraid to die.
He is not afraid of what comes next.
He is not afraid.

Paradise

TESS GALLAGHER

Morning and the night uncoupled.
My childhood friend
who had been staying awake for me, left the house
so I could be alone with the powerful raft of his body.

He seemed to be there only for listening, an afterlife
I hadn't expected. So I talked to him, told him
things I needed to hear myself
tell him, and he listened, I can say "peacefully,"
though maybe it was only an effect he had, the body's surety
when it becomes one muscle. Still, I believe I heard
my own voice then, as he might have heard it, eagerly
like the nostrils of any mare blowing softly over
the damp presence he was, telling it
all is safe here, all is calm and yet to be endured
where you are gone from.

I spoke until there was nothing unfinished between us.
Since his feet were still there and my hands
I rubbed them with oil
because it is hard to imagine at first
that the dead don't enjoy those same things they did
when alive. And even if it happened only as a last thing, it
was the right last thing.

For to confirm what is forever beyond speech
pulls action out of us. And if it is only childlike and
unreceived, the way a child hums to the stick
it is using to scratch houses into the dirt, still
it is a silky membrane and shining
even to the closed eye.

Wake

TESS GALLAGHER

Three nights you lay in our house.
Three nights in the chill of the body.
Did I want to prove how surely
I'd been left behind? In the room's great dark
I climbed up beside you onto our high bed, bed
we'd loved in and slept in, married
and unmarried.

There was a halo of cold around you
as if the body's messages carry farther
in death, my own warmth taking on the silver-white
of a voice sent unbroken across snow just to hear
itself in its clarity of calling. We were dead
a little while together then, serene
and afloat on the strange broad canopy
of the abandoned world.

The Idea of Skin

KATHERINE J. WILLIAMS

           At the hospital
they ask permission to cut off his ring,
then hand me a ragged, split thing
I finger in my pocket, until the day I wonder
why I spared his skin instead of the smooth
cold ring—as though the idea of his body
died a slower death than he, and was still
wrapped about me.

           Time and ashes shattered,
I glimpse myself against the rain in a dark
window, feel my body raw, as if a protective
film I never knew I wore is peeled to expose
the veins beneath. In the harsh light
inside the store, I stroke piles of purple eggplants,
envying the taut skin that protects
the creamy flesh within.

Salvage

JESSICA DE KONINCK

To reverse prolapse
surgeons hold up the bladder
with the skin of a cadaver.

   Science stitches up
   what gravity pulls down.

Cadaver...

More genteel to say organ transplant
better to say donor.   Distasteful

   discussions of corneas, skin, lungs, heart.
   The cash and carry
   business that goes on at night might

get detected. But with casket closed what goes
unnoticed goes unnoticed.

   Picked clean as a car abandoned
   in Camden. Hubcaps,
   headlamps, grill work for sale.

     The business of leftovers,
     like the time we unearthed a steering arm
     and hood latch for the Renault

at a junkyard outside Worcester. Kept
that old hatchback running. So
     at the funeral home I never checked.

I did not ask to look.
With no formaldehyde, wax or makeup,

> a night and a day would only
> make things worse. To the end
> your skin remained taut,
> unblemished, youthful.

> Cancer and infection rot
> from inside out. Your organ
> donor card's a useless stub.

> I did not want to look
>   at you. Contaminated
>   not even good for parts.

The Golem

JESSICA DE KONINCK

I understand the magic of dead things,
the resurrection of mud into matter,
desiring, as I do, to recreate you from clay,
dry grass, beach glass and sand,
wood shavings, graphite, the earth
around your plain pine box. Anything,
to bring you back. Some seed
or pod. Some breeze to breathe
life into you.

I would sit beside you. Breathless,
we would drive away. In our silence
I might forget, golem do not speak,
cannot differentiate the living
from the dead and out of ignorance
do harm. No one in this room
has risen from the dead. No one's
kiss tastes of maggots and ash,

but nothing would stop me
from blending my mortar
of grief and desire to will
you here. I am ready to die.
I would follow you anywhere.

Author's Note: A creature of Jewish medieval folklore, a golem is a figure made into the form of a human and given life.

Cindered

P. C. MOOREHEAD

I am cindered by love,
ashed by it, piled up in charring coals.

No diamond body here —
just ashes, coals, cinders, dust.

Almost a Full Moon

CHRISTINE SILVERSTEIN

Woke up all night long. Finally got up at 5 a.m.
I can feel you all around me.
I can feel the pull of your soul.
I can feel the pull of your love.

Maybe it's that simple. My grief mirrors my love. Oh yes, people who are still waiting their turn chant the "move on and love again" mantra. They mean well. Or they find it satisfying, no, safer, to cushion their dread with optimism. They say, when they move deeper and nearer to the core of life, it's important to love again, to love life. But where they miss the mark is when they think grief must end before life can be loved.

Grief comes to stay. It is a new emotion, a new tenant in your heart with a long lease. Grief is as big and as whole as love. It commands attention. It can ruin your day. Grief takes sadness to new heights and throws it off the cliff. Grief breaks the eardrums of sorrow. Grief takes up residence but with no delicacy. It moves all the furniture around and throws the most cherished pieces out on the lawn. It sleeps all day and parties all night and never cleans up. Grief doesn't pay the rent. It makes us pay.

In the cell structure of our emotional architecture, grief plays havoc. It wears disguises or struts naked, no matter. And yes, it can dull or heighten all the other emotions that make us human. Yet in my new fancy dictionary, grief gets less than two inches and love gets six. See what I mean. Same in life. You are given your whole life to love and are encouraged to shorten the time that you grieve.

But for me it's that simple. My grief mirrors my love.

Solving an Astronomy Problem

LISE MENN

It's certain, as I had always suspected:
You were my sun and moon and stars;
Not one of them rises anymore.

So then, what is that yellow light that heats my skin
And which occasionally warms me for a moment?

It must be someone else's sun that I can see.

It must be someone else's moon that changes shape.
And those must be their stars: faint, blinking, useless.

March Ninth

LISE MENN

The days getting longer, suddenly booted by daylight savings time,
Make me sadder this year. I want to hide in the darkness,
Close the blinds, light the lamps, bury my heart under my work.

Suddenly it's almost dinner time and the sun is bright,
The crocuses are out there, and the tulip spear-tips,
Purple-edged against the brown mud.

I am supposed to be feeling stronger and happier and all that,
But the long beautiful evenings that used to be ours
Stretch ahead of me desolate.

Darkness was better.

Natural Disaster

JACQUELINE LAPIDUS

After you died the planet cracked and flooded,
tourists swept away by tidal waves
in Asia, the laughing city of New Orleans
reduced to rubble and mud. Every newscast showed
survivors stranded on rooftops waving
crude signs begging for rescue.
Such devastation swamped my own small grief,
but the day your so-called friends gathered without me
to bray about your wonderful life,
I sat huddled on the sofa as the snow fell.
I did not care at all about the refugees, or global warming.

You, no doubt, would have got on a plane
to report (though not to do) what could be done.
You would have teased their stories out,
black grannies coughing as they were carried
from the boats, children without shoes. Yet their dead
were no deader than mine as I cried for you,
dear stubborn foolish man
who dragged heavy furniture in from the porch
and refused to ask for help.

What Happened After

JACQUELINE LAPIDUS

In memory of Edward P. H. Kern (1925–2004)

I.
The undertaker's parlor on Union Street
was bare and honest as a pine box. He spoke with us
kindly in his Navy sweater, remembered who
you had been and did not retreat
when I told him about the lawful widow.
Of course she put on the customary show,
shedding crocodile tears for the benefit
of a minister you had never met
and what she had of you went into the meadow,
but she never found out a secret share
was kept aside for me.

II.
All winter the house lay under snow,
snow, three-foot drifts blocking all doors
and cutting off the road. The dented Subaru
slept in the garage. Come April, when
Nantucket turned to mud, that demented dragon
swooped in again from her distant mountain
and stripped the space of everything you loved—music, books,
beds and rugs, porch furniture, piano, old maps
from the stairwell basket, those beautiful antique lamps
that were your mother's—and the great table
where only the summer tenants ever ate.
Thanks to the will, I got the car out.
Your father's Oxford oar went

to your nephew, your clothes to Danny
who found you on the floor.
By the time I returned to scatter your ashes,
only the view was left.
                                   I stood, bereft,
in the meadow facing Coatue and wept,
then picked some daisies for the Harlemans.
Everyone who cared came with me to Madequecham.
And by end of September, Don was dead too.

III.
We say the dead have entered into rest.
Back in the city I go out at night
looking for peace in some dark place
without lights, so I can see the constellations.
Now that my navigator's gone, how
will I know what to call them?
These oceanic tears would make both Dippers
overflow, dim the Dog Star, rip the diamonds
from Orion's belt. Dearest, greatest, best, last and henceforth
constant lover, watch over me until we are reunited.

Widow's Litany

ROSALIND KALIDEN

Widow.
Dirtiest word
in the English language.
Dirty word in any language.
Curse.
Punishment.
Social declass.
Social demotion.
Mariah.
Pariah.
New leper.
Invisible woman.
Behind orphans.
Below divorcees.
Bottom of the pecking order.
Object of sorrow.
Object of pity.
Object of laughter.
Object of derision.
Object of dismissal.
Object of inferiority.
Object of scorn.
Easy target.
Easy scapegoat.
Most vulnerable.
Free fodder.
Free candy.
Undefended.
Indefensible.
Disrespected.
Unprotected.

Laid bare.

Widow Laments at the Ice Gate

HELEN RUGGIERI

the fire dragon lives under the ice gate

No sun comes here
long winds from the north breathe
the dragon's name in the language of weather
we no longer speak

Snow falls on the mountains
fills the laps of valleys
where the woman waits.

She has not heard
her husband's voice
in a year,

nor seen letters
of his hand
arrive at the gate.

The miserable cold
picks at her bones saying
he won't return.

An empty hollow
in the wide bed
they shared.

Easier to bridge
the river with stones
from the mountain

than to cut away longing
and snow falling
snow falling.

Too Much Life

IRIS LITT

Could I ever make poetry
out of that crash
of metal against stone
that smash of bone and flesh
that took the scurrying days punctuated with laughter
and the wild firelit loving of evening
that had nevertheless very much to do
with babies?
The only poetry
is those babies who
transplanted still like male trees kept growing
and I unwillingly living beyond
that crash in the matter-of-fact morning.
I am coming
eventually to where you are
but not to join you, my love, as we planned.
You left too much life in between,
too many babies,
too many evenings
in the morning of my life.

In the Rain

PATRICIA L. GOODMAN

Dread precedes us like a dirge
as my daughter and I
walk the edge of the woods.
We have found his note.

Dave! I yell. My voice shakes.
Don't, Mom, she whispers,
you may startle him.

We enter the tree line
near his deer stand.
She extends her arm to stop me.
Ahead, beside the tree,
a yellow mass of rain slicker
on the ground.

It's Eric, she breathes,
our youngest son,
a crumpled ball of despair,
beside the body of his father.

Valentine's Day

ANNE CAIRNS FEDERLEIN

Valentine's Day was always my favorite until my husband shot himself in the head at exactly 2 p.m. and I became a widow.

Henry was a successful lawyer in a wealthy Detroit suburb. I was the president of a small university campus in Ohio.

He left no note. An e-mail, written at 3 a.m. said happy valentines day, all in lower case with no apostrophe. His last call was to the inside line at my office as I was driving home to celebrate 38 years of marriage.

At exactly 2 p.m. on that fateful day, I drove into our driveway just as Henry was parking his luxury car at a nearby boat launch. He leaned on the hood and fired a practice shot. Then without hesitation, he placed the gun behind his right ear and fired again. A policeman patrolling the beach heard the first shot and screamed, "Henry, stop."

Later as the policeman was searching the car, he inadvertently hit the cell phone and redialed the last call. When I listened to messages three weeks later in my office, I heard discussions about registration of the gun and what size plastic bag to use for the body.

I felt nothing. I agreed to funeral arrangements that anyone wanted and somehow stayed in a presidential mode, stoic, rational, and articulate. Or so I thought. My assistant took care of me. She drove all my black suits and shoes to Michigan in a blinding snowstorm. On campus, she relayed a story about my husband's heart attack to the board. Without knowing, she saved my job.

After the funeral, I found bullet shells on the bedroom rug and bags of shredded paper in the garage that were our financial records. Henry's expensive suits and 200 white and blue dress shirts still hung neatly over thirty-five pairs of Italian handmade shoes.

My friend of twenty-five years never called. She told a mutual friend, "he was my only close friend. I want to die, too." At that moment, I knew they had been lovers.

I spoke to no one for two weeks. I sat at the kitchen table staring at a crystal bowl filled with rotting fruit.

The gun Henry used belonged to our son.

My dear New York friend never left me. She discovered I was $500,000 in debt, had three mortgages on the family home, fifteen credit cards with high balances, an emptied IRA account and no life insurance.

When I finally went to Henry's office, the lawyers closed their doors. I saw a copy of our trust on the corner of the desk next to a framed picture of a baby I didn't recognize. His partner was waiting for me.

"Henry was under investigation for fraud. He illegally invested our retirement contributions with our stockbroker by using his license. Every year at tax time, he returned the retirement funds plus one percent. Profits made were split with the broker. Last year they shared $35 million. When the market collapsed last week, Henry knew it was over."

The bookkeeper in the firm, a former cleaning lady, handled all of Henry's accounts, paid our bills and practiced my signature on many documents. The book *Accounting for Dummies* was found in her desk drawer.

The suicide was never reported in Henry's obituary, only his accomplishments.

Five years later, on Valentine's Day at 2 p.m., I was fired as president.

My Husband's Bones

JOANNE SELTZER

The partner who danced me
off to whatever life would bring
lies in a simple coffin
among an old man's dental shards
and relics classified as bones—

bones unadorned by skin,
unconnected by flesh,
untouched by fire, unscattered
to the four corners of the earth—

bones the Valley of Death will hold
until time shatters and Adam's
DNA is a broken cord—
bones that may rise again
or not—these are my husband's bones.

Learn to Love the Trees

ANN MCGOVERN

I was city-bred and knew only weed trees.
When we married, we moved to the country.
Learn to love the trees, he said. Call them by name.

He tacked labels on tree barks—sycamore, larch, maple, spruce.
He taught me their names and I spoke to them.
In the winter, they cut silhouettes,
their smell was snowy sharp, their bark a harsh touch.

One year he died on a windy, wintry night.
My trees swayed and bowed and moaned till morning.
I buried him in a box made from a pine.

So now what is left of that tree?
Without light and air,
without someone calling its name?

Remorse

ELLEN PECKHAM

From habit, overwhelmed, distraught
dropping "…personal effects…"
I go to wash

then realize, despairing,
I have erased from my fingers
your tears wetting them as I closed your eyes,

cells gathered as I stroked your face,
last oils from your hair,
destroyed our last exchange,

our last intimacy mixing all uniquely us.
If only I had thought to take a veil to hospice and,
like Veronica, pressed it to you,

a piece of silk prepared to gather
dear invisible harvests.
If only I had thought ahead!

i am sure

CAROLYN STEPHENS

i am sure

life would be better

if i could sleep

more than two hours
at a stretch.
if i did not fall asleep
every single night
light on
book in hand
glasses perched on face
heating pad for company
and letterman in the room with me,
gap-toothed grin
so like J's,
and then wake up
every night
for years now
always at three
—the hour he left us—
regardless of
what hour i retire,
what pill i take,
(or what we forsake).
tv still on
celebrity poker now
toxic
all those comforts
no comfort at all.

i wander the house
in the darkest hour of night
staring out blackened windows
onto wet pavement,
wind-whipped leaves.
there is still
a big hole
in the bed.

Bereaved

KATHARYN HOWD MACHAN

Her husband turned to silver, burned away.
For months she couldn't make herself believe.
She'd wander home, drink wine at end of day,
stare into dark as though her eyes could weave
a shroud that she could pull apart by dawn
to bring him back, lone hero, from the cave
where shadows rule. Sometimes she'd walk the lawn
beside his garden rows, where he once gave
her tongue a first tomato, perfect, red
beyond all fire's crimson, that hot night
so many years ago. And what he said?
Our love will last as long as there is light....
She's learned to hate the mornings, flow and ebb
of time a dull bedraggled spider's web.

This product is licensed to Liz and Paul von Transehe

ELIZABETH VON TRANSEHE

This life was licensed to you and me!
It says so.
On the computer when I turn it on,
On the papers to our house.
On our marriage license,
On the birth certificate of our child.

On our plane tickets,
On the car payments (the car we fought about),
On thank-you cards we sent out to friends (Love,
Liz, Paul, and Zoe).

On my memory
and my body
and my soul.

It's written there!

We signed together.
I don't want it alone.
That is not the deal.

You are my emergency contact.
This is the emergency!
My life is burning down!

Boats

DIANA O'HEHIR

I'll write, Bill yelled
waving
as his boat accidentally broke loose from the pier.

He wasn't a lover, just a good friend
and we got him back in half an hour
but he did write
often

and I've got picture of the boat
a plastic skiff
with a blue stripe.

I also have a photo of yours—your boat

a small white yacht
which steamed purposefully out into the bay
and stopped to let you off.

You and I and our son were on it.

I leaned against the rail
while Michael upended the black ceramic box
which held the dusts and gravels of you.

How did you know that was him? someone asked.

I said I didn't.
But really I was sure.

Your colors were gray and white
with an orange flower floating in the middle.

Goodbye darling, I said
I'll write

as you swirled symmetrically away

beyond the views of Marin and bridge
toward Tiburon

where we used to live.

Thirty Years

DIANA O'HEHIR

You said, *I thought of you every day we were apart*
and we were apart
thirty years.

I laughed and told you that was impossible
I tried to pull your hair
which was white and clipped short.

Your son and I discussed this
at your deathbed
over your prostrate body.
(You were quiet
being full of morphine.)

And once again I said, *Impossible*
not every day
not for thirty years

which woke you out of your coma.
You struggled up
and tried to say, *yes*

propped on one wobbly arm
on the too small
rented hospital bed

Yes.

while I moved toward you
just beginning to understand
how thirty years
is not that long.

Not compared with
permanent.

Not compared with always.

The Widow of Few Tears

BARBARA L. GREENBERG

1.
How is she doing? Has she
begun to weep? Not yet, but she is
walking back and forth in

coastal waters
which are composed
entirely of tears.

2.
When she is offered body parts—
arm, hand, shoulder, lap,
breast, heart—

the quiet widow, the amputee,
rises to embrace
her would-be donors.

3.
The widow of few tears
releases one
into the steaming pot.

"Taste this soup,"
she would have been saying to him.
"Does it need more salt?"

Some Kind of Widow

BONNIE LOVELL

After my divorce, I often traveled to Mexico. At the border, on the tourist card's marital-status box, I never checked "Divorciada." I always checked "Soltera"—single. Once, an immigration officer, filling out the form for me, misunderstood and checked "Viuda"—widow. He smiled sympathetically. I didn't try to explain. It would be easier if I *were* a widow, I thought. I had never wanted to be divorced, even after I knew it was inevitable. I imagined saying, "I'm a widow." But I wasn't a widow; I was a divorcée, divorced, *divorciada*.

And now that my ex-husband has died, my second thought—after *Make it not true!*—was *I'm a widow*. I remembered a scene. Where had I heard it? "*Seinfeld*"? Somebody—Elaine?—was ranting about a divorced acquaintance who was going around after her ex-husband died calling herself a widow. Elaine was enraged. "She's *not* a widow!"

And I'm not really a widow. There's no word for what I am, no box to check to describe the nuances of my marital status, the limbo to which Jim's death condemned me: Once married, now divorced, with a dead ex-husband. Some kind of widow.

Just as no word exists to describe what I am, no one knows how to react when I say my ex-husband died. A quick, "Oh, I'm sorry," followed by a pause, a frown of concern and rapid change of subject. Yet I am in mourning. I need someone to listen to me wail, keen, curse the unfairness of fate. I need for my grief to be heard.

It's true: we divorced. But, once, we loved each other; we were happy. We hated each other; we were miserable. We loved and hated each other, often in the same hour or minute. Sometimes, I confess, I wished he would die. Death would be so much simpler than divorce, I thought. But when he did leave me, briefly, before our final breakup, and drove to L.A., I couldn't sleep for fear he'd meet a bad end, wreck the car, die. I didn't want him to die.

And now, long divorced, I counted on his friendship. I wanted him there, reliable, safe, at the other end of the line for our comfortable chats. I wanted always to hear his familiar voice, his chuckle. But now he's dead.

While Jim was alive, even though there was no chance we would remarry, the book wasn't closed. As long as he was alive, I could cling to the irrational belief that our story might turn out differently. I wanted a happy ending. Now time has run out. We will never have another chance to make it right; there's no other possible ending: We married. We divorced. He died. I will never have a lifelong marriage. So I'm mourning not just my ex-husband's death but also the death of our marriage and the hopes and dreams embroidered around it. When I help scatter Jim's ashes in the East Texas Piney Woods, I will finally let go of all that—of my youth, of lost dreams, of our past. The wind will do its work and carry them all away.

With friends like these...

JACQUELINE LAPIDUS

She says *I don't know what to say,* as if
she'd been raised in the woods by
wolves. Did he leave you anything?
Now he's at rest, he's with God, I'll
pray for him. He wouldn't want you to
feel miserable, why are you wearing
black? Here, have a drink, it'll cheer
you up. You're lucky he didn't linger.
Can we talk about something else? But
he gave you so much grief! But you
weren't even married!   When you
start dating, will you be looking for
men or women?

To My Well-Meaning Friend

RUTH S. ROTHSTEIN

To my well-meaning friend who said:
You must be relieved that your husband is dead.
And you must feel guilty, of course.

I think it's you who's relieved that my husband is dead
And you who feel guilty for that.
You can breathe freely
You've been released
All images of suffering gone

But I'm now imprisoned in hell on Earth
My climb has only begun.

Ashes

KRISTINE SHOREY

December 2, 2008, late afternoon on a San Clemente beach. I'm here to memorialize my first husband, Kurt, who died 20 years ago. With me are my bridesmaids, including Kurt's three sisters. The air is cool and we are alone.

Twenty years ago on this day, Kurt died of brain cancer. He was 33. I was barely 29. We were married only a year before he showed symptoms, which took another six months to diagnose correctly. After that, for the two years he lived, I refused to consider he might die, although we no longer spoke of the future. His last month, he could not speak at all.

The morning he died my family was with me. I watched as if from behind a glass wall as they took it upon themselves to remove signs of illness. My father threw all Kurt's medications into a garbage bag. My mother had the rented hospital equipment removed. My sister vacuumed smooth the dents the hospital bed had left on the carpet.

By noon my mother had a cremation service on the phone. "Where do you want the ashes scattered?" she asked me, phone to her ear.

"Over the ocean, where he used to surf," I croaked.

"They can do it in Long Beach." She lowered her voice and added. "You don't even have to be there. No reason to put yourself through that."

I should be there, I thought. But because at that moment I could barely imagine leaving the house, I just numbly recited my credit card number, and it was done.

As I emerged from my daze in the following years, those ashes haunted me. As the 20th anniversary of Kurt's death approached, an idea came to me. I could create ashes out of something meaningful and scatter those. But what to burn?

"Why not write your regrets out on paper and burn those?" suggested a chaplain friend.

And so on that beach we are gathered around a bonfire. We tell stories of Kurt's quirks and kindnesses, his facial expressions, the growly voice he would use to make us laugh. One by one, we light tiki torches and say what we miss most about him. We write our regrets, crumple them up, and throw them into the bonfire.

As I watch the flames consume the paper I realize that without a shovel we will be unable to scatter the hot ashes.

"The wind will scatter them for us," his sister says, pointing to the bits of ash already being lifted by the breeze. I am unsatisfied, angry at my lack of foresight, my failure, after all of this, to do what I came here to do.

I leave the group and walk out to the water. Staring at the waves, an image of a grinning Kurt bobbing on his surfboard comes to me. I wonder what Kurt would have said about my planning failure.

"Hey, don't worry about it," he says in his funny husky voice. "They're just ashes."

The Widow Takes Delivery of His Ashes on Beacon Hill

GAIL GILLILAND

The mortician delivered your ashes today—
Green box, gold seal, like a Christmas gift.
They weighed more than expected in my hand
And I wanted to tell you that the neighbor you called "the Nazi"—
Because he policed the street for garbage and unstickered cars—
Had heard me call to the mortician when he arrived:
"Mr. Spencer? Just pull up on the sidewalk over here!"
The Nazi cried: "Oh no you don't! We don't want people
Pulling up on our sidewalks to break the bricks!"
After the mortician, a Southie, had parked his van,
He walked over to the Nazi, pushed his Irish face up close to his
(It was scarred—but from what, I wondered, a burn?)
And said: "Where I come from, Mister,
People show a widow some respect!"
I didn't mean to collapse, but did.

I used to tell people I would never be lonely,
Never be bored, that not even
Life in a nursing home
Would make me flinch.
"Just give me a library," I bragged,
"A pad of paper, a pen, and I'll be all fixed!"
It isn't true, I can tell you now.
I'm scared as hell. I don't know where you are,
Why you don't walk down the hall
Wearing your old blue sweater with the leather sleeves
And sit down across from me as I try to read
And interrupt me again and again as you always did.
I promise I won't be cross if you try again.
I won't give you that look: *Now what?*
I made you so lonely
And that breaks my heart.

don't

SEREN FARGO

don't tell me you know
you don't
don't recite quotations of comfort
they are not
don't demand my happiness
loss does not bring this
don't tell me not to mourn
it is how I move through grief
don't compare my loss with yours
I am not you

Refractory

CAROL TUFTS

The Stages of Grief:

> Denial
> Anger
> Bargaining
> Depression
> Acceptance

I cannot let go, cannot
follow the protocol, refuse
closure, refuse to doubt you
are about to slip back through
a loophole, undo the tricked-out
trickery of the spring your heart shut
down in the willful green of the thick
coming grass. I rage at you now as I did
not rage then. How could you
have left me to the futile pink
of the Red Bud preening
like a buffoon through the glass
of our bedroom window? Look:
I stand ready to make a deal.
Take what you need, then call it quits
with eternity. I know you grieve, too.
I will never ask another indulgence
from whatever it is we end by
calling upon *in extremis.* But you do
not, will not, did not, come back
for all this time I pass confounding
assumptions, eluding the rules
for healthy adjustment and getting on
with the rest of it I still cannot accept.

Counterpoise

CAROL TUFTS

I wish I could still feel you gave a damn,
lurking like a voyeur, never deigning
to drop a clue, not even when I try
to draw you out with a dumb show,
or a straight line. This is one of those
fundamentals that takes longer
for me than most to master,
like the way numbers ascend
on a clock to add up to sixty,
or no matter how you face it,
the needle on a compass trembles,
always stopping to point
due north. The fact is you
dead never return, not ever
with the serendipity of spare change
and lost dogs. And I do
hold forth until I am blue
in the face, exhuming consolation,
burrowing in to hollow out
a channel to float you back through
the unmapped latitudes of my grief,
even as the ratcheting days wash over
your traces and the nestled press
of your limbs against mine gives way
to the cat caressing the space
where you lingered, a phantom
who would refract the darkness,
a breathless whisper to raise me up
to that frequency I cannot sound,
perfect though I may be,
tuned to its pitch.

Cremains

CAROL TUFTS

(for Bob)

You hold on that spring like the blossoms
of the Red Bud against our bedroom window,
their tenacious pink fading
only as the leaves pierce through
and you lose yourself
to a terrain so clear cut
it breaks your heart,
fills your eyes
like fathomless inlets
impervious to light.

Returned to me in fragments
like tumbled stones, or crushed shells
marooned by a receding tide,
you arrive cut to fit the solicitude
of a mortician's euphemism,
shards I gather in my hands
to set adrift along the fluent
bruised Maine coast
where the sea lays down
its cold, its salt.

the sun holds no sway

ELIZABETH PAGE ROBERTS

the sun holds no sway
                              has no power to move
                    even the miniscule in me
        i am not touched
by even the edges
                    of time or the sky

there has never been
   an empty
so full of nothing
   so deep with endlessness.

                              in the contemplation
            of years
                    and minutes
                              a life of these
it is here
        that the missing
                              (a chasm opening further into nothing)
      defies imagination
                    eludes grasp

there has never been
   a solitude
so solitary
      a grief so paradoxical:

      weighing like the volume
              of all earth and days
                                        but in the stillness
                    of any now

i feel you have not only
never left me
but have indeed
entered me entirely

How Could I

PATRICIA SAVAGE

have known
that trusting calm
and reason would leave
you unescorted
out of this life
and find my nose
now pressing
against the cold pane,
straining to watch
what I then could not,
them taking you
out the front door
zipped up
in black plastic.

I had turned toward the light,
the children in the kitchen,
bound to the care of the living,
choosing alchemy to create
cold sense out of the molten
lead of your passing.

As the world forgets,
my turncoat heart laments:
how did I not grab
at their heels,
screaming?

Wonderland

GAIL BRAUNE COMORAT

The year her husband died, snowstorms followed
in the wake of his burial. Two-day events,
not the brief glitzy whirl of a snow globe, but snows
that shrouded her landscape, obscured the rows
of azaleas they'd planted that spring:
lovely and terrible. She was shaken,

transformed. No longer a wife.
Now a widow, a single parent in a topsy-turvy world.
Displaced, sliding through time, suddenly
she seemed the largest in a crowded room,
too small when alone. Was everything temporary?

By day, she was blinded by an ever-present glisten.
At night, the Cheshire moon dazzled her,
dizzied her all the way down her rabbit hole.
I've had nothing yet… I can't take more.
She waited for the thaw. ›

But when March hurried in with more pale mornings,
she stepped through the door once again
into white-gloved quiet, the only sounds
her scraping shovel
and the slow-motion crackle of brittle glass.

Do You See What I See?

CHARLOTTE COX

This sleek little six-seater plane
gathers speed, leaps into air,
leaving summer treetops behind
on its way to escape from real life.

The rippling depths of aqua,
turquoise, indigo, below us
steal my breath, spin my head,

and I turn to see if you see
how beautiful the moment is—
but there's just an empty seat.
Anyway, you would have said,

"Oh, beautiful? That's too easy,
you romanticize everything,
tell me what you really see."

So beauty's not enough for you—
you want reality? How about
the choking sounds at 3 a.m.
I heard beside me in our bed?

How about my frenzied call to 911
with the phone clamped to my shoulder
as they instructed me in CPR while

my fingers pinched your stubborn nose,
my lips forced breath into your mouth,
my fists pounded hard and urgent
on your chest—too high? too low?

My eyes would rather memorize
the azure layers of this lake,
the sandy shores of this island.

While yours, I suppose, will keep
the white light of God or crematorium
as their last sight. And yes, I know,
we always did see things differently.

When one door closes

"M"

The door is round and open. Don't go back to sleep.
—RUMI

Nick is naked when they storm the door.
I struggle to cover him as though he is a virgin
in the temple of Vesta. I needn't have bothered.
They brought the sheet—white cotton,
meager thread count, standard size for beds
and bodies. I sew a sail of that cloth
with the needles he left behind.
Set him to sea like a chieftain on a boat,
Francesca says, but ships won't sink
on city streets. I give him to strangers instead,
transfixed until the van's doors slam shut.

I am that metallic sound, a failed provider leaving him
in the cold with the thinnest of fabrics, no coin
in his mouth. The entry to our home remains
ajar for days, a broken yew strewn across
the threshold. When that passageway closes,
I tell Francesca I am the traitor who deadbolts
the door against a husband unfaithful
enough to die. *What else is there to do*
when it is cold outside, she asks. In my hand
is his band of gold, their archaeological find.
I swallow the ring. It cuts through the larynx
gone tight in my throat, and in my stomach
it turns round, full, and open.

Shoes brought me to this place

"M"

I slip through rooms in black felt
clogs many sizes too large and *n/um tchai*
until dawn. They force me to breakfast
with the others, tell me to eat institutionalized
eggs if I wish to be whole. *Scrambled*
is good for me? Scrambled was the van
that carried me here. My fork shakes
like the *shekere* I bought from a Nigerian man
who whistled through his harelip
and taught me how to dance.

The woman who eats my eggs
draws balloons on my breakfast tray.
The reason you can't fly is you're too attached
to the mass of artifacts. I tell her it is the pull
of shoes. She says we are all addicted to something.
I use her pencil to sketch shoes
on her bare feet. She turns into someone else's
conclusions. Her balloons rise like a hallelujah,
and flee for the window to the outside.
The strings tied around their necks
tangle in my hair, taking me
closer to the sweaty woman whose eyebrows
crawl up her forehead like caterpillars
to cocoon in her hairline.

She has some authority here.
She wants my shoes. I tell her they are not mine
to give. She kneels at my feet
to remove them. I bite into the sunburn
on the back of her neck. I eat, sleep, bathe

in shoes. When the shrieking starts
late at night, I hide inside them, soft
and safe. They are risk, ritual, reward.
He is dead, the therapist tells me.
No, not if his shoes still dance.

Author's Notes:
n/um tchai: !Kung medicine dance, done for healing and to ward off evil.
shekere: Percussion instrument consisting of a dried gourd with beads woven into a net
　　that covers and surrounds the gourd.

Mourning

JACQUELINE LAPIDUS

Living in Greece I learned
why so many women wore black:
a year for parents, for a husband
forever, telling the neighbors *take*
care of me, I am weak with grief,
I have turned to ash inside.
The clothes made each day easier, everything
matched. You, like most New Yorkers,
hardly noticed how long I wore black
for my mother, black is what
everyone wears. But when you died,
my friends here found it morbid,
year after year a shadow of my former self.
You would have been the first to say
isn't it time to stop now?
A smoky scarf, a lavender top,
my summer whites and finally, last fall,
Mom's tailored brown tweed suit.
I had gained so much weight, it fit me.
Now I can wear sage and lime, I can imagine
this summer in pastels, but yellow, red
and coral hang in the closet, too painful.
I try, then put them back.

Grief Becomes Me

DONNA HILBERT

You've never looked better,
my friends Edward and Neil
tell me and lean close
for a clearer view.
I know what they mean
and believe it's true,
the same way earth and sky
wash to a radiant clean
after relentless days of rain.
How you would present me
with pieces of sea glass
tumbled smooth
from journeying canyons
and rivers to the ocean
and back again
washing up at our feet—
bits of amber, green,
and the rarest stellar blue.
Everything pure and impure
has leached from the soil
of my face,
and in the corners of my eyes,
hard crystals form.

Lesson

DONNA HILBERT

A portion of ashes we buried,
the portion remaining to be scattered
sits on a shelf
in my office, the container swathed
in a flannel bag, like the bag
protecting your tuxedo shoes.
How handsome you were in formal clothes!
Strangers often asked if you were *someone*.
Should they ask for your autograph?
The irreducible things that make up a person—
ashes, bits of tooth and bone—
transform from one noun
into another.
Before your death, Dear Heart
I didn't know
that physics and grammar
are the same sad subject:
the transformation of matter,
transforming what matters.

Secret Society

ALISON KEELER CARRILLO

It's hard to be a widow.
People are afraid of me.
They don't know what to say.
Who knows what to say?
I don't know what to say.
I'm speechless most of the time.
Instead of asking, "How is your grieving coming?" which is relevant
anyway, they will talk about anything else to distract from their
discomfort about not knowing what to say.
I feel for them.
It's most awkward.

Some people do say, "How are you today?"
What I love is, "Oh my dear, I'm so sorry you lost your sweetest love."
That makes me cry and then you can hold me and I feel better.
We are closer and you have helped me at a hard moment.
All moments are hard because I am constantly reminded that he is
gone. What do you say in the face of such a brutal reality?
Say, I'm so-o-o sorry, and then touch me.

This widow's road is incomprehensible.
I had no idea.
It's beyond the beyond.
It's another world.
It's an experience of the other world.
It's a secret society, hidden.
Who wants to feel such a great loss?
No one, we hate it, we want to keep it hidden.
Mom said, some women would be glad if their husband died.
Not so when a woman has lost her true love.

After nine months when the shock started wearing off and I began
feeling worse, Pam said, "Oh, you're in the abyss."
"The abyss," I said, "there's an abyss?" I've heard about it, is this
it, this feeling of freefall down a black hole where I have no idea
where I will land? "Yeah," I said, "that's where I must be, in the
abyss."

Every morning I wake up and fall farther.
Oh, this again.
Night is the high point of my day when I reconnect with Ed.
I remember a dream where we were lying together and I was begging
him, oh Ed please, can't we be together in some way, can't we at
least be lovers? He closed his eyes and enfolded me in his arms, no,
my darling, not now.
I sobbed as he rocked me gently.

It was hard enough for him to die.
For him to stay dead is my outrage.
Every day he is dead again.
Every day I remember.
It still is shocking.
Dead?
No!
Impossible!
Our life was my life, how can it be over?
And there is nothing I can do but submit to the vicious truth.
By nightfall my horror is complete and has broken down to resignation.
I surrender to sleep, the blessed balm, and into the arms of my beloved.

This much I know.
If you want to comfort a widow there are four things that make a
difference: show up, hug, listen, and cook. Don't get me wrong, cards
are nice, especially as they evoke memory and tears. If you want to
feel better, send a card or call. But if you truly want to comfort
your friend, show up at her house, listen to her, hold her in your
arms. Give her a safe place to weep and rage. She used to sleep in
the arms of her beloved, now she is alone. She will get used to this
soon enough, but if you can, spend the night, stroke her, sing to
her. This is your beloved sister who needs you right now. Do you
know how deep is the love you are showing her? Do you know how much

she appreciates your being there and how strong is the bond you are forging? Yes, you do, because you too have suffered or know that you will soon enough.

The truth is, this is a solo journey.
There is nothing anyone can do.
That is the frustration of it.
If only there were a pill, a platitude.
But no, there is nothing but to weep and dream.

A Widow Learns

LENORE MCCOMAS COBERLY

not to live without him
but to live with him.

The stair that squeaked
when he came down from his
hideaway office still squeaks.

The pace of a solitary walk
is measured to his stride,
observation is double.

As shock wears away
rich memory, unbidden,
comes.

II
Memories, Ghosts, Dreams

Memorial Day

CHRISTINE SILVERSTEIN

Memorial (n.) "Something that serves to preserve the memory of an individual or event."

Day (n.) "The time between sunrise and sunset."

I mowed the grass on the circle at the end of our dead-end street yesterday, rearranged the bench which sits alone adorned with the carved Sergeant's chevron in the wood, planted flowers in the chunky clay pot, and thrust two flags into the ground—Old Glory and the Nantucket Police—and then stood out of breath and windswept to take it all in. It's the last day of May in the last few days of the sixth year that I have spent wishing this never happened.

If only it were that simple to preserve the memory of you between sunrise and sunset.

But what about the deepest night? The random clap of thunder? The damp, clammy feeling behind my neck when I can't sleep? What about the startling recollections of something funny you did while I'm staring at the produce display? What about the grapefruit-sized lump in my throat that appears out of nowhere when I'm in a meeting to discuss sewer districts? Does all that count?

Most would say I need psychiatric attention at this late date. Still living the hermit life, pining after you, surrounded by memorials, and wishing in my heart of hearts that you would just pull into the driveway this morning, let's say in about an hour (I can be patient), after debriefing from the midnight shift, and the sound of those boots on the steps downstairs would be the next sound I hear. Wishing in my heart of hearts that you would climb the stairs and I'd be able to feel the palpable exhaustion in every step knowing how you would be looking forward to a huge hug from me and the feeling of our bed underneath your weary bones. Most would have me locked up.

What if that something that serves to preserve the memory of you is me? What if I am the flag, the flower, the monument? Does that count? Does that validate my sanity? What if the last drop of the soldier's blood sanctifies the ground it fell upon and the last brush of your lips on my neck sanctifies my flesh?

Does that count as something?

Poignant

JUDY BEBELAAR

I think I understand
what the word means now

since I passed that corner
Irving and 19th
and for a small part of
perhaps a second
a flash in my mind
or heart
I thought I'd be able to turn and
go to the UC hospital
where my husband worked
pull into the parking lot
behind Langley Porter
and he'd be there
with his curly brown hair
give me a kiss
and we'd go off to the beach
or out to dinner and

I could almost feel
our lips touching

when I realized
all this in less than a second
and I didn't even
really believe it
as much as see it
a quick scene in a movie
of course
it was impossible

John had been
dead for more than five years now

and that is why they call it
poignant
like a small cut
poignard
a small sharp knife

Snapshot

BARBARA BALD

She knew the moment she met him
that she would want to show him off,
carry his picture in her wallet
like a young bride, sticking it
under every stranger's nose.
Look, she'd be saying
with her eyes, *see who loves me?*

A real man's man, old George would add,
About time!
Strong, broad shoulders, muscles that bulged
when he stacked wood,
gristled carpenter hands that veined
when he swung a hammer,
wide arms that offered protection in every hug
and wry, dry humor that promised tomorrows.

She didn't know then about his other love,
the one who secretly demanded all his time,
occupied every waking moment,
often rendered him unconscious.

She tried sharing him with her,
tried forgiving human frailty
and her own fears of letting go,
tried ignoring garbled words and strong hands
lying listless on the couch.

She lived with bottles hidden in drawers,
his head occasionally bobbing over his dish,
cigarette burns in the kitchen linoleum.

Watching his strength dwindle,
labored breathing taking its toll,
she sobbed when she found him lying near the bed,
glass mistress by his side.

The wallet-sized photo, yellowed with the years,
rarely leaves her purse now,
but daily she whispers his name.
Look, she is quietly saying with her eyes,
see who once loved me?

Memory Foam

PAT PARNELL

It seems like forever
since you've slept in our bed,
but our mattress remembers.
It saves your place,
a long, narrow trench.
Like a grave.
I'm solitaire, as the song says,
"sleeping single in a double bed."
But our mattress persists:
cohabitation.

It raises a ridge of firm foam
between your side and mine,
won't let me sleep in the middle.
I keep sliding in my sleep
sliding down my side of the ridge
sliding back into the hollow
shaped for me
so many memories ago.

Sometimes I wake in the dark,
know the weight of you next to me
in your own space beyond the ridge.
I feel your warmth, breathe your scent…
then I remember.

Flashback

PHYLLIS WAX

I remember those legs
bare
tempting
next to me
at the breakfast table

the warm
muscled
right thigh
my left hand
couldn't resist

Departing

PATRICIA SAVAGE

I don't look
at photographs.
I stare at them
held so close
my eyes bore
through paper to skin,
skeleton, sinew.

It's not memory
I am after but feel.
I miss your feel,
your flat hand
on my back,
then squeezing
my shoulder,
then folded over
my own hand
while we sink
into the sofa.

Marriage is hot baths,
marinara sauce,
cookies, farts,
noisy yawns,
garlic breath.
It's small redemptions,
embrace, expressed
gratitude bringing us back
home every evening.
It's my chin on your head
while you read Paul Krugman,

a foot rub for my pains,
your toe nail scratching
me while we sleep.

You are taking
so much with you,
sweet nothings, pet names.
Lying sideways, you'd say,
See how well we fit?
Our legs stack,
your bowed shins,
my knock-knees.

I give you to the fire.
I cannot bury your body,
have it still be here,
even though
you're done with it.
I am not done with it.
I am not done with you.

SEREN FARGO

death anniversary—
the rain clouds outside
make their way in

spring cleaning—
deciding to keep his shirts
one more year

Feeling the Hollowness in My Chest

MARCI MADARY

At the movie theater
    and we didn't buy popcorn

On the Saturday morning
    when I only took one coffee mug from the cupboard

At the restaurant
    as the man leaned over to greet his wife with a kiss

When the clock chimed nine
    and I didn't hear your keys turn in the door

As I looked out the window at the flakes of snow
    and knew you wouldn't be calling
    to say that you loved me.

I Want to Ask You

JESSICA DE KONINCK

Do they ride motorcycles in heaven?
like the Suzuki you drove to Cape Cod and met me in the middle
of the night, or the BMW you rode with your brother
from France to Egypt, then from Nevada to California to bury
your father, or the one you saw crash and the rider quivered
on the car hood where he landed, and you did not ride
after that? Your bike remains in the garage.
I have not moved it.

Maybe you get a new Harley in heaven. Doesn't need gas.
Never breaks down. Easy Rider, I hope you chose a Ducati,
your favorite, something with class, expensive, or an Indian,
sleek and speedy, with deco letters, the kind they don't make
anymore. Perhaps it has a Cupid face and heart-shaped
fenders like the Valentine you drew for me.
I kept that too.

Better than wings I think, a two stroke, or a four stroke, faster,
more comfortable, more maneuverable. You can park it
outside. Wings would be clumsy, weigh you down.
Not like a bike. Your helmet, your saddlebags,
your black leather jacket, I kept everything.
You still flew away.

Pillow Talk

JESSICA DE KONINCK

Sometimes I cannot wait to die
    just to sleep next to you again.

Some nights I will be the one with cold toes,
    some nights you.
We will take turns
    cold toes to warm thighs.

At the burial I worried.
    Perhaps you will not like the Rosenfields.
    After all, we never met them.
Even if they do not argue
    there is so little room.

If only you would dig yourself up,
walk back home, all bone,
    a bit of flesh,
    a tuft or two of hair or beard,
    and talk to me.

That would be enough.
    I would fall asleep.

Come Saturday Morning

REBECCA SCHENCK

Before we knew you had cancer, I was planning to write a poem about our enjoyment of going to the Farmers Market. The title would be "Come Saturday Morning" and the last two lines, "What would the other one do / if we were no longer two?" We had asked that question.

If we were in town on Saturday, of course we went to the Farmers Market. Longtime vendors knew that we would pick the vegetables with unusual shapes or colors that matched our pottery: red onions, turnips and eggplant. We said we were picking produce to use first as centerpieces and later as food to eat. We described the Mr. Froggie wedding breakfasts we had in our hollow tree, serving three green beans and a black-eyed pea on each plate. Sometimes cucumbers and gourds took the natural form of animals, which you loved tucking under your arm. When the offerings became more routine, we still relished buying what was being sold by people we had come to know and admire.

The last time you were there, Mrs. Hoffman walked you to the car that I had pulled up close to her booth. A couple weeks after you died, I took her your obituary, told the berry man and the flower man, didn't buy a thing.

The second time I went, Nise was back with her spring lettuce. When I told her you were gone, she hugged me and cried, handing me a mixed bag of red and green. She told me Lily had lost her daughter. I didn't recognize the name, but she's the artistic woman who placed flowers beside the little vegetables on her table. I stopped to sympathize with her. Mrs. Hoffman gave me a jar of jelly and mailed me an Easter card.

Another week I bought one tomato, one bell pepper, four yellow squash and a $2 bunch of blue ragged robins from the Asian family we liked so much. Gas prices are going up again, and I stopped on South Tryon to fill the Volvo. A woman at the pump noticed the flowers lying on the front seat and said they were pretty. I told her they were our favorites but my sweet husband had died; then I burst into tears. She said, "That's all right," and I said it wasn't.

Last Saturday I went to the Farmers Market again. When Mrs. Hoffman gave me pink peonies, I remembered your mother talking about the peonies that bloomed the May you were born. At the plant shed I bought two Irene lantanas and stopped to tell the Celtic herb man that this year we have a full crop of his Kentucky Colonel Spearmint, but you are not here. He was so sorry and handed me a pot of dill.

I came home and had what we liked best for a summer Saturday lunch: an ear of corn, a BLT and iced tea with a sprig of mint. I miss you.

Phantom Limb

LAURA MANUELIDIS

You are my phantom limb
Cruelly disjointed, cauterized,
Vaporized beneath the hot iron. I dream

I can rivet you whole to me
Again when death is near
To rush through the fields of gliding green

And meet, where the wind still blows
An oboe reed, imperfect as the voice
Though I can't hear your half footfalls

For they are soundless as your vanished thoughts:
The ones I cannot speak
As grass flies through my feet.

I see my mother with a parasol,
My father in his white summer ducks
About to row the round-bottom boat
Under the bridge where we used to go Sundays
In the Brooklyn Prospect where they once kissed.

And you seem just as close,
Almost reached, like them
In the Botanic sunset where I run

Impossible to wake any more.

Author's Note: Phantom limb: when the brain acts as if what's lost is still attached.

Chora

LAURA MANUELIDIS

I am dancing for you
Only for you, Elias
The way I used to
On your birthday
Eyes open
While yours are now closed.

No one has called today.
It's too long ago.
Besides
Laertes doesn't like Rembetika
   "Too guttural and crude," while
Manolis never even listened to them.
They are in ancient Sapphic stanzas
The sounds you can't translate
From the archaic.

How is it possible to experience joy
When tears pulse through the floor
Only to be swallowed?
How is it possible to remember pine trees
Disappeared from the shore
Last winter
Or comprehend their pointed light that pierces the past, scented?
The pausing wind, the boughs outstretched,
The invariant
Syncopation of fingers—
Snapping.

My feet are lifted and simultaneously embedded in the ground.
How is it possible to still dance for you

Sitting in that empty chair
With every feature of your head present
Like granite?

The musician's pick is laughing
While the strings incessantly repeat refrains of
Αγάπη,
The mystery.

Author's Notes:
Rembetika: harsh songs, exposed without craft, written by outcasts between 1820 and 1930
in Lydian, Dorian, and other minor modes, mainly syncopated against the heartbeat. A
few are in perfect Sapphic stanzas.
Αγάπη (agapi): love, in Greek.

Until

LAURA MANUELIDIS

I weep uncontrollably only to myself.
When I speak to you it is in the ever-present tense:
Others require the past. Separate ashes.

For you are here weeping with me although I cannot touch you.
You are like the wind that fails to find its cradle in the naked tree
You, who blew across my green body for this timelessly short ecstasy.

Once there were stars at night as we slept entangled
Now when I wake, there is less than the absence of light.
Nothing moves when the wind has no place to put his head.

Give me back those textures where I have no right to dwell
So I can pause within your eyes. To not be banished from your lips.
To float upon your breath, to ride the sky.

No, this Odysseus is not coming home
So I must wander centuries furrowed in an olive pit
Until death rejoins what it asundered:

Then the world can squander itself again. As if love free.

January 2007

JACQUELINE KUDLER

This morning I remember to wash my hair
and I am separating tangles between
my fingers. A fat sun, squeezed between
the rim of the window shade and the low black
cloud on the horizon, warms my face,
but you are not here.

You are not here easing the *Chronicle* out
of its plastic sleeve, scanning the sports page,
laying it flat on the kitchen table, and you are not
parceling out the vitamins at your place and mine.

You are not downstairs at the fish tank
tapping out food flakes on top of the water,
and you are not slumped at your desk in
the swivel chair, squinting at bills, or stretched
back in the Lazy Boy arguing with the a.m. news.

The low cloud rises to cover the morning,
and shrouded in shadow now, I pull your
green chamois shirt around my shoulders,
but you are not here.

Not at your chair at the kitchen table,
not bundled in your half of the bed,
not on your side of the living room couch,
and you are everywhere

but you are not here.

Old Woman Dreams

PATRICIA FARGNOLI

He came to her finally in his torn jeans and soft
tan jacket, came from feeding the horses,
their sweat still on his palms,
came redolent of hay, honey from his hives—
Solomon's Song on his lips.
Came with the old scar on his cheek where
she left the chaste imprint of a kiss.
Younger, impossibly younger,
he told her what she wanted to hear.
But only in dream, night, the color of his black hair.

Around him, her arms wound like his branches,
his eyes were a garden she ached to lie down in.
They met in a wind-rush, and what she remembers
is a craving to follow where he was leading.
Also the impression of dissolving
against the astonishment of his chest.
Her desire seems to have its own life and will not be
expelled no matter how often she tries to banish it.

Somehow an old woman feels all this. Is it so odd?
She's heard a dream embodies a message
from the totem spirit, like the fox
who emerges in flame from the forests
and goes to hide in the morning hours.

Who Will Not Be Home

"ARIEL"

I can't wake from the nightmare you are dead.
I dream of you
smelling the forest on your skin,
have conversations we never had,
like last night's conversation on the history of our valley;
who owned the land before,
what they farmed,
your Washingtonian twang posing questions
as you do when your country mind ponders and dreams,
holding my hand as you drove
your thumb brushing against my palm.
It was Halloween, the smell of fallen leaves and wood smoke
combined in the car with your immediate scent,
strong like it has been every year.
We talked about who will stay and who will not be home,
who will open the door.
You pulled into our driveway in the afternoon light
and then asked our son to park the car.
Now it is morning and I wake still to winter's chill,
an empty bed,
fall still eight months away;
your absence from my dream a sharp pressure,
my lungs emptied of you.
I throw my arm over my eyes
trying to will myself back into the dream
but I already know the futility of it;
there is no more conversation with you
You now exist only in pictures, in poems
and dreams.
And I must live within this nightmare.

Ghost Dream

DONNA WAIDTLOW

Friends kept telling me
I dreamed of Richard last night
It was so vivid
I was jealous
Have you forgotten me so soon?

Then I dreamed you:
I walk into a hotel room
The bathroom light shines behind the closed door
Someone is there
I feel it and fear tights me

The door opens, closes, opens, closes
I know now you are teasing me
But my heart is still pounding
You are, after all, dead
These four long years

The door opens
Laughing, you emerge with your arm
Around your father's shoulders
You say, *My Dad and I have been trying*
And trying to reach you…
We need to tell you…

The image wavers, curves
collapses on itself

I'm instantly cold awake
Wrapped in blankets

Thinking: What? What? What
Was so important
You had to journey from beyond
To tell me?

What? What? What?
Could you just come back
Hold me
Finish your sentence?

Waking the Dead

JILL JACKSON

"All Hallows Eve" last night.
You did not awaken although your shadowy spirit lingers everywhere.
Ironic…
You used to hate Halloween:
Your imaginary finger pointing, *"j'accuse!"*
all that American fascination with horror and ghoulishness.

Growing up, my brother and I used to enjoy the fun, the dress-up,
the greetings of mock fear at our "trick or treat" mantra,
the warming hot chocolate while Dad culled the sweets he liked best.
No parents trailing us to ensure untainted bounty;
things were apple-bobbing simple.

Now, I want answers from you.
Did you meet a deity today, or ever?
What color is the aura of God (if there is one)?
Did you change your opinions of Halloween,
of Americans and their propensities,
of good and evil?
On which side of the spectrum do religions fall?
Is your soul in some laughing or colicky infant?
Is your presence, which I feel,
my illusion, my consolation?

Is there a God?
You have so much to report now,
why are you silent?

Left Behind

BARBARA J. COLLIGNON

Hammer on the landing
pliers on the floor
drill bits on the windowsill
paintbrush near the door
trowel here
garden gloves there
I can trace your footsteps
attic to cellar
driveway to garden
by what you left behind
as though you planted clues
for me to find
to be certain
I will follow

Shaky All Day

PATRICIA WELLINGHAM-JONES

I ambled into the hospice shop
(donated a bunch of stuff after Roy died),
hoped to find a table
for the new guest room.
At the end of a rack of clothing
lurked a special rack of better things—
four of Roy's summer shirts ($3 each)
and the red plaid flannel ($4)
he wore the week he died.
Those shirts, empty of life,
draped, listless, on hangers.
I stumbled around in tears,
got out of there.
Shook for the rest of the day.

Circumflex

NATASHA SAJÉ

I gave away his clothes, keeping
only wool I could wear, a hand knit
sweater, natural grey cream—

February 27, his birthday, now gone a few weeks
and forever, like the battle of Hastings

where English shields couldn't hold
and the language also gave way

after 1066 the circumflex appeared in
certain French words—*trône, suprême, voûte*—
an ornamental sign of grandeur

indicating not even absence

together we saw the Bayeux tapestry
in subdued light behind glass in quiet rooms
marveling at detail

a thousand plus years later

will I see someone on the street wearing
the blue checked shirt
with rough weave & bone buttons I liked so much?

signs are vacant seductions, it's him I miss

in French a missing "s" can be marked with a circumflex

like the roof of a house in Ceyras, Languedoc:
constellations of crosses on doors
and beams scratched with the year

a thousand plus years ago

when animals lived below their owners
and village houses crowded together against
attack, within town walls now gone

in one-third of the population
the left ventricular circumflex supplies
the sinoatrial nodal artery

in others blood takes a different route

his body presses memory

festival becomes fête (*fête d'anniversaire*)
paste becomes pâté (how we loved to cook)

the vowel, then, of a certain quality, and long

alphabet comes after sound
as clothes make and do not make a man

winter is winter
no matter whom or what
I miss or gave away

Bureau

HOLLY ZEEB

Plundering your cache
of balled-up socks, I caress
the rough softness of wool, cotton,
ribbed and smooth. Little wads
of black cycling socks—your fleet life.
Bundles of worn, work-a-day socks—
for digging, planting, harvesting.
At my finger tips no silk, nothing
fancy—only small mute animals
huddled for warmth.

Cold Tea

HOLLY ZEEB

Chamomile, solace of insomnia—
this remnant of last night's

falling into sleep—
soothes my early waking

from dreams of you.
There on your side

of the bed, a pile of books
to weight it down, keep you

from leaving during the night.
What do I care about the world

these days? *I do, I do.* But how
to find my way beyond the mind,

the steadfast heart of you?
At night I hear you breathing,

deep enough to enfold me in your sleep.
Yet these early mornings, the day steals

even as it slakes the thirst of wanting you.

Receipt: 11/07/09

HOLLY ZEEB

From your pocket
this crumpled slip:
red leaf lettuce,

cucumber,
yellow pepper,

avocados (on sale),
grape tomatoes
(two for one—you,

always a mark
for a bargain).

You were traveling
by bicycle, the one
you fell from

two days later. Always
your saddle bags full

of food or books.
Did we make a salad
that night? Guacamole?

You, peeling and chopping,
our voices mingling,

red wine swaying
in our glasses. I hope
we savored, laughed.

I can't seem to stop
sifting through clues,

winding myself in the past.
It was Saturday—
were we expecting guests?

Ghost of Prescott Park

BARBARA BALD

I saw you in the park today, walking amid tourists
enjoying ocean breezes,
apple blossoms raining scented petals.

From a distance I knew it was you:
smoke-colored canvas coat, faded blue jeans,
tan leather work boots splotched with paint,
salt-and-pepper hair that never obeyed a brush.

You walked, paced, retraced aimless steps,
round the docks and back again,
round the docks, back again.

It was your form that gave you away,
eyes to the ground, shoulders drooped from
demons you carried in your pockets,
cuffs too long from Jack Daniels tugging at your sleeves.

My eyes followed every step, watched you stop, stand awhile,
look at families pushing strollers, friends playing Frisbee.
I imagined you wondering why this life wasn't for you.

I remembered days we talked together, laughed at jittery spaniels,
sat by a rocky river, built cabins in our dreams.
Staring at you, I tried to savor the strength, the illusion
of safety I felt when we walked arm in arm.

What do we do with memories that
wear familiar faces, images that flood over us,
catch us unaware, memories that sleep in locked rooms,

light us up from the inside out,
stir feelings numbed from years of trying to forget,
ones that sit beside us in our cars, place smiles on our faces,
then leave us sobbing at the wheel?

I knew this wasn't you, couldn't be you, but I wanted it to be,
wanted to get it right this time, to stroke your hair,
meet you at the door, asking *How was your day, dear?*
I hungered to ease your pain.

I wanted this to be you until I heard the stranger mutter
to himself, *I want some peace. I want to end this hell.*
Grateful you'd been released from such agony,
I said a prayer for the man I thought I knew.

Seeing you tip your head forward, like a hundred times before,
place your back against a tree,
cup your hands to shelter a cigarette from unwanted breezes,
I lingered awhile, then left.

Somewhere

JANE HAYMAN

You have been sleeping now for over three months. Sleep is what Merwin calls it in his poem *Good Night*. "Sleep softly, my old love," he writes, "without end in the dark."

You are my old love but I don't think you're asleep.
If you are, it's time to wake up.

Poets speak of death as "sleep" and "night." Dylan Thomas called it "the darkness of the darkness."

I would rather think of you in heaven, your kind of heaven, which I picture as The Ramblas in Barcelona on a sunny October day. You are sitting at an outdoor café, talking and laughing, drinking beer, and smoking one cigarette after another.

Each cigarette is stamped: *Good for celestial health. Increases wingspan and strengthens flying ability.*

Post-Mortem

JANE HAYMAN

The phone rings. Hello hello. It's your ghost again.
Every day letters from you in the post again.

I told you to leave but there is your face
when the fog floats in from the coast again.

Here by the fire, there by the stair.
Go back to your best in the frost again.

Stay out of my mirror. This is goodbye.
Forget my address.   Get lost again.

The Acropolis Diner

HEATHER CANDELS

Our menus flopped open
and we looked
but ordered the same thing every time
Me, hard eggs,
You, corned beef
Us, whole
wheat toast, coffee, cool water
ice cubes jingling, melting.

Our future sat near us
in the red vinyl booth
cozy like the bowl of oatmeal
on the counter, still time
for raisins, sprinkles of sugar, or a trickle
of syrup before it got cold.

Sweet roll
aroma curled around us like kittens.
I swizzled cream into coffee
while you buried yourself
in the sports pages
where every day was new.

Sometimes winners lost
and sometimes losers won.
Stadiums went up,
and stadiums came down.

Stavros barked orders
over his bushy mustache,
ripped off tickets

clipped them to the wheel
for short order
cooks ready to flip
today's specials.

Plates slid off his arm
like colorful Cadillacs floating
down a parade of promise
gliding right onto our table.

And we ate, never paying
attention to the taste,
or the sugar that sat in the bowl,
the syrup that hardened in the jar
the sweet raisins we left in the box.

Peeking through those windows
now that you're gone, I see
a blue interior, higher prices
no sign of Stavros.

Still, the hash keeps frying,
the eggs keep breaking,
and that smell lingers when someone pushes
open the door.

Memorial Candle

FLORENCE GRENDE

The spent candle, housed within a midnight blue glass casing nine inches high, stood guard on the fireplace mantel for one year, surrounded by our family photos. It belonged there, as you would have belonged near our son gleefully holding on to his graduation cap (it was a windy St. Paul day and you would have been shining with pride). It belonged there, as you would have, among your three daughters sprawled on a black and white lawn; among my parents, unsmiling eyes wide at our wedding; and among your grandchildren shyly posing in vacation swimsuits. I positioned it closest to the photo I snapped of you before we married, holding on to the ropes of a sailboat, your cap at a jaunty angle, your face lit by that familiar gap-toothed smile. The photo of my mother at age 80 flanked it, radiant in a pool as a dolphin planted a kiss on her cheek. The candle burned for seven days of Shiva, the traditional mourning period. I hadn't touched it afterwards

Until now.

One year. A marker. Am I now to begin life anew, cast aside the candle like yesterday's news? Is there a cutoff date for grief? One year and turn a page. Get on with things.

No. I can't discard it. My grief not yet over.

It's just a candle, I think, removing it from the mantel. I peer inside. A dead fly curls near the wick, its legs question marks.

This past year, days rolled into weeks.

Weeks bled into months.

During those months the spent candle became a touchstone, grounding me in your absence, reminding me of my inability to cry. Reminding me that loss can also be dry, residing in the crusty interstices of winter, in the numbing silences of our now too-large house.

I won't cast it away. I'll place the candle deep within the shadows of a lower shelf. Hidden, like grief.

Those Days

MARY OLIVER

When I think of her I think of the long summer days
    she lay in the sun, how she loved the sun, how we
        spread our blanket, and friends came, and

the dogs played, and then I would get restless and
    get up and go off to the woods
        and the fields, and the afternoon would

soften gradually and finally I would come
    home, through the long shadows, and into the house
        where she would be

my glorious welcoming, tan and hungry and ready to tell
    the hurtless gossips of the day and how I
        listened leisurely while I put

around the room flowers in jars of water—
    daisies, butter-and-eggs, and everlasting—
        until like our lives they trembled and shimmered
            everywhere.

East Avenue Gulf

MARILYN BATES

Richie kissed the starchy pavement,
when the ozone cracked a comma in the sky
and the mole on his neck took root, sending him
to soil he loved so well. Like a lit fuse he gardened
with a fury around the Gulf station he ran like a pit stop.

Now, nothing stirs in the darkened building.
Gas pumps seem beheaded. Graying aluminum hangs
a dirty bib around a garden that is no more.
The only movement, a note flapping on the door
thanking stranded patrons he rescued on the highway.

I gauged my safety by the vigor of his hair, watched
it wane from roan to dun, imagined serrated blocks
of chaos when they'd take the building down.
No more bougainvillea on the trellis, forked tongue
of iris, or bees sucking larkspur. His obituary
hangs on my refrigerator, as if evoking luck
when on the road alone. I touch it in passing.

Gone

ANN MCGOVERN

How could I lose the name of a city,
a town, a whole country and a river.
What was that city with its gold museum,
its grey sky and the chill.
Shanties tilted on hillsides
and higher still, grand mansions.

And that pastel town—what was its name—with its steep streets
that would have left me short of breath
had you not placed your hand on my back

to help me climb.
Where was it that you picked
yellow daisies, rosemary, and Queen Anne's lace?

Wildflowers, you said
for my wild woman.
In Ireland, what was that river where we slapped

mosquitoes on its banks and embraced
on a blanket so thin
the sharp grasses scratched our legs.

Ten months later, you were dead.
Only then did I remember
Lima, Cuzco, Portugal, and the River Lee.

The Weight

ANN MCGOVERN

Objects remain.
Baskets bought in Borneo
the day we saw the deadly snake

on a river trip, coiled
in a jungle tree above us.
"You die before you scream," our guide said.

A Turkish rug from Istanbul. We looked
at a pile of hundreds. We might have curled up
on the bottom, smothered in history.

A Vietnamese medicine chest
I use for jewelry, one drawer
for the earrings you gave me.

How can I forget the countries where we bought them,
the shops and the shopkeepers,
the ways I thanked you for each lovely pair.

But mostly, your leg against mine,
for instance.
The shocking weight.

Maybe You Are Here

ANN MCGOVERN

Maybe you are here after all.
Ask the Mexican sun.
There is no calendar that marks your death.
You signed no contract for immortality.

Yet here in San Miguel, church bells
ring your name from dawn to deep night.
You are the courtyard treasures
hiding behind carved doors,

the lush orange trees,
the feathery fountains.
Inch by inch I seek you
among the cobblestones,

feel your skin on textured walls.
In this high place of steep hills
and dry wind, my breath struggles,
never wanting any other air

except that which you breathed.

Literal

DIANA O'HEHIR

She said, I felt as if half of me had been amputated
I know that's how you feel
not literally, of course.

She said, certain experiences will bring him back
gusts of music
or warm spring air.
They'll bring him back

of course, not literally.

But why not literally?
that's what I really want.

To open my front door
that gasps when it's pushed

and: *Enter You*
grinning a success
I knew I could do it
I knew WE could do it.

You smell of
whatever Jesus smelled of
myrrh or frankincense
or some such.

And arms held wide
and big, big grin

(that's you, not Jesus)
and big, big hug

The literal you
so real it hurts.

Why Can't I Dream About Him?

DIANA O'HEHIR

Seventeen months and still not back
He must be having
   a tough trip.

A friend said it's a short drive
I know better; it's
   hard days, harsh nights.

He'll be here
   if I just give him time

Someone saw him in Santa Barbara
I know better; he's
   over the border.

Someone glimpsed him at the Picasso show
Send me directions, I said
   I'll go there too.

A letter told me he's surely forgotten
I tore that into
   tiny scraps.

A friend said I should face facts; I said, no
Facts don't count when you're
   waiting.

I'm not worried, I told them all, I know
there are people
   some people
   just a few

come rain or sleet or flood or snow
that always follow through
    that simply don't know how
    to let a girl down.

He'll be here soon.

Crazy Menu

TESS GALLAGHER

Last of his toothpaste, last of his Wheat Chex, last
of his 5-Quick-Cinnamon-Rolls-With-Icing, his
Pop Secret Microwave Pop-
corn, his Deluxe Fudge Brownie Mix next to my
Casbah Nutted Pilaf on the sparser
shelf. I'm using it all up. Chanting: he'd-want-me-
to-he'd-want-me-to. To consume loss like a hydra-headed
meal of would-have-dones accompanied by
missed-shared-delight. What can I tell you?
I'm a lost proof.
But something eats with me, a darling of
the air-that-is. It smacks its unkissable lips and
pours me down with a gleam in its unblinkable eye, me—
the genius loci of his waiting room to this feast of rapidly
congealing unobtainables. Oh-me-of-
the-last-of-his-lastness through which I am gigantically
left over like the delight of Turkish

Delight. Don't haul out your memory vault to
cauterize my green-with-moment-thumb. Or shove me
into the gloom-closet of yet another cannibalistic
Nevermore. I've been there. And there too. It was not
unusual—that bravado of a castrato in a brothel
yanking his nose and waxing paradisal. No, I'm more like
a Polish miner who meets a Chinese miner at a
helmet convention in Amsterdam. Because we both
speak a brand of Philip Morris English picked up
from a now extinct murmur heard only impromptu
at a certain caved-in depth, we are overwhelmed by
the sheer fact of meeting and we clasp
each other by our bare heads for nights, exchanging

the unimpoverishable secrets of the earth, the going down and
the coming up, the immutable pretext of light, a common history
of slumped canaries, of bereaved kinfolk, of black-lunged
singers and handmade coffins. We trade
a few eulogies and drinking songs and sit down at last to
a huge meal of aged cheese and kippers.
We lean into our vitals

with all the lights off. It's dark inside and out.
This is our last chance to revel in the unencumbered
flickering of Balinese tapers we bought at
a souvenir stand above the canal. Like rice and spit
we are tolerant of all occasions, this being
the lifting of the dread whereby
the girls' wings we autograph onto our duffle coats
have been painted like butterflies, only
on the upside so the dark is mocked by
our raised arms, our fluttered concentration, uncollectable as
the lastness I am of him I love-ed
scribbled unsentimentally on a valentine in 1983:

    To the King of my Heart!
In daylight we pick up our tinned rations and hike off,
every artery and nerve of us, into the rest
of our commemorative lives.

Ring

TESS GALLAGHER

Not the one he's wearing in that stopped length
of ground, but the one we saw together
in the little shop in Oregon—moss agate so green
it was nearly black on its silver band. Hard
to come across it after, emptied of his hand
and watchful. Thinking to surprise its power
with treason, I gave it to our friend who wore
no rings and needed its luck. But soon I knew,
don't ask me how, the ring
lay among lesser things in a drawer. I asked

for it back, and for a while, wore it on a chain
around my neck. But it was awkward
like a high-school charm, the sign of love a girl
outgrows—not as it was, exchanged for the rose-gold
of wedding bands. Where is it now?
In some abject safety.
But where? Put away. I turn the house upside down
searching. Not to find it—worse
than omen. Like happiness squandered in fountains
with wrongheaded wishing. Or the hit-and-miss

taunt of memory, its dulled signature so casual
it crushes me lucid and I believe what I don't believe
in the way of true apparitions—that he uses
my longing to call himself to me,
that my senses are inhabited like the log
into which a bear has crawled to dream
winter away, that the ongoing presence of the dead
is volatile, sacramental. The wind he's
attached to—that boy, running with a kite over
the gravestones, looking up, keeping his footing

as if he worked sky into the earth with
a cool boldness. So the dead-aliveness of my love
turns in the flux of memory, of what his memory
would recall, as he is recalled
to a street in Oregon, dead and alive in love,
with the strangeness of cold silver
close around the finger on his new-made hand.

Deaf Poem

TESS GALLAGHER

Don't read this one out loud. It isn't
to be heard, not even in the sonic zones
of the mind should it trip the word "explosion"
and detonate in the silent room. My love
needs a few words that stay out of
the mouth and vocal cords. No vibrations, please.
He needs to put his soul's freshly inhuman capacity
into scattering himself deeper into
the forest. It's part of the plan that birds
will eat the markings. It's okay. He's not coming
that way again. He likes it where he is. Or if he
doesn't, I can't know anything about it. Let
the birds sing. He always liked to hear them
any time of day. But let this poem meet
its deafness. It pays attention another way, like he
doesn't when I bow my head and press my forehead
in the swollen delusion of love's power to
manifest across distance the gladness that joined us.

Wherever he is he still knows I have two feet
and one of them is broken from dancing.
He'd come to me if he could. It's nice to be sure
of something when speaking of the dead. Sometimes
I forget what I'm doing and call out to him. It's me! How
could you go off like that? Just as things were
getting good. I'm petulant, reminding him of his promise
to take me in a sleigh pulled by horses
with bells. He looks back in the dream—the way
a violin might glance across a room at its bow
about to be used for kindling. He doesn't
try to stop anything. Not the dancing. Not the deafness

of my poems when they arrive like a sack of wet
stones. Yes, he can step back into life just long enough
for eternity to catch hold, until one of us
is able to watch and to write the deaf poem,
a poem missing even the language
it is unwritten in.

Dream Doughnuts

TESS GALLAGHER

for Maya

Mother, I'm so glad
  to see you again! for she had been dead some while.
Oh my son! she says, kissing him, I'm also glad
  to see you!
I have so much to tell you, he says.
  Tell me, then.
Not now, mother, he says. *We have so much time.*

At the Parisian restaurant Pierre tells his dream
of meeting his dead mother. Sebastian, the jazz musician,
says he's giving up drink, going to take better care
of himself. It's time he *found a nice girl and settled down,*
had some children. Two young mathematicians at the table
discuss logic, which I'm always hijacking
with metaphor and image. I tell them how I read Ray's
book of poems cover to cover until he entered
my dream as through some side-door in the jazz club,
some loophole in time.

I'm so glad to see you again, I say.
He's carrying a bag of powdered doughnuts
and two paper cups of black coffee.
Was I gone too long? he asks, fresh from the bakery.
Too long is if you don't come back at all, I say.
Time is funny, he says, biting into the doughnut
so the hole breaks open to the entire air supply
of the planet. Powdered sugar clings to the corners
of his lips. *Ghost-lips* I call him, as he

tears off doughnut and feeds it to me like a small bird
who won't eat any other way. Time,
like the doughnut hole, has rejoined itself,
as when joining breaks us open to ourselves, corollary
to again.

I say to Ray:

> *Did you ever think*
> *it would be like this?*
> *Drink your coffee,* he says, *while it's hot.*

For a while we're all out there together, but soon
I know I'll have to go back to that alcove
in which we're always waiting to see
each other again, the one we call Life, so it has
a hole in the middle, a sign of arrival, given
so we don't need to miss ourselves or anyone else,
we're that sure the whole,
in some unaccountable lightning-flash-hyphenation,
goes on and on, as it takes
our very breath away.

Deshacer

DONNA HILBERT

I open the garage door
and our dog bounds free
across the street,
disappearing down the alley,
her black form unmade
by the moonless night.
I panic, run in circles with the leash,
but you calmly cross the street
calling her name.
Because she loves you
she lets you bring her home.

I won't repeat the dream
in which you leave me.
Let's just say I know the world,
how it alters in an instant,
that I awaken sick
in remorse and dread.
I can't face again the dinners
with other lonely women,
then late-night TV
until the dog and I can bear
to go to bed.

I don't need again to learn
the bitter lesson
that everything I love
is a flame between two fingers,
no act undone, no word unsaid.

The Wild Things

T. J. BANKS

(for Tim)

True to form,
      you didn't make your good-bye
            an easy conventional one:
a rain-slick road a hard-to-handle van
            & you were hydroplaning
                out of my life
                out of this world
                with a sound & a fury & a violence
                    that tore my heart apart,
                    scattering the pieces
                        along the asphalt.
The skies opened,
taking your quicksilver soul up,
      leaving behind a crushed & bloody shell,
      not the body whose lines & moles I knew
            like my own.
Weeks after you died,
a deer came to the edge
            of your garden
the sensitivity you hid
under your Tim-foolery
      staring out of her eyes
      as soul met soul in gentle greeting.
And only days later (so it seemed),
a hummingbird flew up to me
moving through the heavy late-summer air
with a joy & lightness so like yours....
No conventional good-bye, no:

but you spoke to me
       in the language we shared
       our love of wild things
sending me messengers
who could reach me
       when no one else
           could,
letting me know
you'd fallen
       in a good place.

Waking

MAREAN JORDAN

In the liminal blue dawn
grace note between sleep and waking
I rest in the dream's arms
and there you are
guide across the great divide
where nothing dies
and the world's made new
all salvaged
all forgiven.

October 26, 1991: Outside Saratoga Springs

SANDRA M. GILBERT

Unseasonable heat, as I slip toward
Eastern Standard time, below a rank of rusting
east coast trees not far from where
six years ago we quarreled, kissed, gave thanks.

Sun cooks a small polluted pond
you'll never see, coated with curled-up
leaves the local sculptor wants to use
as models for her "floating baskets."

The water's dense and black, as if this lake were
what they call a *tarn;* the trees
lean in, companionably blackening themselves.
Back home, in burnt-out Oakland, an older widow

asked if I "felt a presence."
No I don't. I always hated Halloween,
the fat dead pumpkin with its silly mask
of life, the kids pretending to be ghosts,

the mockery of skeletons. Down here
among the shredded leaves, the rocks are only
rocks, the shreds just shreds,
and the fish that leap in the murk

probably don't know they're "leaping."
Your eyes are gone that might have loved
the last quick lights in these Berkshire trees.
Something turned you into a stone of yourself.

What baskets of wishes
can I even dream of fashioning
to float next week across
the chilling waters of All Souls Night?

November 26, 1992: *Thanksgiving at the Sea Ranch, Contemplating Metempsychosis*

SANDRA M. GILBERT

You tried coming back as a spider.
I was too fast for you. As you
climbed my ankle, I swept you off, I ground you

to powder under my winter boot.
Shall I cherish the black widow,
I asked, because he is you?

You were cunning: you became
the young, the darkly masked
raccoon that haunts my deck.

Each night for weeks you tiptoed
toward the sliding doors, your paws
imploring, eyes aglow. *Let me in,*

Let me back in, you hissed,
swaying beside the tubbed fuchsia
shadowing the fancy cabbage in its Aztec pot.

And you've been creatures of the air and sea,
the hawk that sees into my skull, the seal that barks
a few yards from the picnic on the shore.

Today you chose a different life, today
you're trying to stumble
through the tons of dirt that hold you down:

you're a little grove of mushrooms,
rising from the forest floor you loved.
Bob saw you in the windbreak—

November mushrooms, he said,
off-white and probably poisonous.
Shall I slice you for the feast?

If I eat you, will I die back into your arms?
Shall I give thanks for God's wonders
because they are all you, and you are all of them?

The meadow's silent, its dead grasses
ignore each other and the evening walkers
who trample them. What will you be,

I wonder, when the night wind rises?
Come back as yourself, in your blue parka,
your plaid flannel shirt with the missing button.

These fields that hum and churn with life
are empty. There is nowhere
you are not, nowhere

you are not not.

February 11, 1994: Berkeley, Anniversary Waltz Again

SANDRA M. GILBERT

The year revolves toward pink and red,
toward the tiny Valentine
hearts of the plums,

each blossom a pink frill
and a core of blood, a frill
and its bloody core. . .

Three times the nurses wheeled you into the icy room,
three quarters of your life just barely over.
Three years since you set out for nowhere,

three years I've studied these blossoms alone,
the indifferent flush, the roseate
aplomb they set against bare blue.

To have gone on becoming without you!
Three nights now since we met in sleep,
and I told you sorrowfully

that you were dead—
three nights since you wept in rage,
lifted your handsome shadowy head and howled.

But how your face has changed!
You're beardless and pale,
a different man, a *spirit* man

as if when we were spun away from each other,
as if when I took my first three giant steps
into another somewhere,

you too could never be the same,
you too had to go on becoming
and becoming other,

becoming alone. . .
As if the only February thing
that's sure to be the same

is still the plum tree's
blind pink three-week waltz
with air and light and darkness.

Apart

ALINE SOULES

I've given you away.
I don't know who got
your lungs or eyes or
bones, but your heart
went to a young woman
with two small children.
She wrote to say that it will
slowly give way to her body's
disease, but not before
she sees her children grow.

Are you breathing in the chest
of a man just down the street?
Do you look at a lake
through the eyes of a boy
who has only known
the sound of its lapping waves
or the chill of his first
plunge of summer?
Can you climb a mountain
in the now-sturdy legs
of a woman on the other side
of the country?

The more those legs
take you away from me
and your heart pumps in another,
the more you breathe
to a different rhythm
and each of us sees people and places
the other will never know,

the more my empty heart
wonders if we have met again,
neither of us able to recognize
that we are together still.

Ours

LENORE MCCOMAS COBERLY

It was an ordinary late afternoon
when he came from our living room
into the kitchen where I was making
bread & butter pickles and said
he could not bear this place if
I was not in it and I turned
to see the naval officer he was
returning from the war and when
he kissed me I felt a magic I
knew he felt too. We were
outside ourselves, together
in a place we did not name,
yet knew it to be ours. Swaying
to a rhythm only we felt, we smiled
before he returned to our ledgers
and I to our bread & butter pickles.

People urge me to go to the cemetery
where they say I will find him,
but they are wrong. He is not there.
He is in our yard, in tedious ledgers
he left well tended, in my memory
that transforms grief
into love and pickles.

As the Crow Flies

REGINA MURRAY BRAULT

If I don't call you don't lose faith
when you break down my garret door
expecting to find a skeleton still clutching
her pen like the spoon that fed her soul.
Look for me instead
where the black crow circles
casting shadows on thick moss
and where summer webs
like spun-lace doilies
drape a granite stone
to snare the bees.

I'll still be in a skin
stretch-marked from weight
of three moon-babies in my belly
and wrinkles
where some capricious crow
did a buck-and-wing across my face.
There will be faded stitches
the shape of railroad tracks
that lead to pillaged places—
a writer's bump
a wedding band.

I will be lying to his right
like a missing rib
separated by inches
of cherry wood and ruffled satin.

But if you climb this ancient path
to find me

I'll know you're here.
Like moss-protected soil
that feels the shadow of the crow
I always know
when someone's standing in my light.

Ghosts I Have Met

MARIANNE BETTERLY

When we bought *Ghosts I Have Met*
at Moe's bookstore on Telegraph,
we giggled after reading the first page,
vowed to read one page aloud
every night before bed.

Not that we did.

I didn't know that in twelve years
I would be in bed, alone,
reading that book to you.

You entered the world
of mist and lights,
sudden breezes closing doors,
before I was ready
to say goodbye.

We still see each other in
shadows and dreams,
but bodies make things happen.

I understand the Buddhist phrase,
precious human body,
now that I no longer can touch your fingertips,
feel your naked chest against mine,
whisper in your ear,
hear you chuckle.

You cannot warm my pillow—
even if you heat my heart.

Maybe you can help me write
a new page about the other world—
where you go when you are not with me,
how it feels to pass through walls and mirrors,
become the wind,
float across the pale sky.

Honey Bees

MARIANNE BETTERLY

The bees returned
the same day
he left me a widow,
on the sixth memorial,
bitter day of days.

At first I thought
they were monarchs
filling redwood branches
with flutter
but in the golden light
their wings glimmered
crinkled cellophane,
as they sped
in and out of leaves;
ten thousand bodies
madly whirling
until sucked into a tarnished gold
vibrating ball —
a pulsing heart
throbbing for the new queen.

The bees first appeared
five weeks after he died,
swarming onto a branch
outside our bedroom window
near the empty hospice bed.
They pollinated my clover for a week,
while I whispered Buddhist prayers
for a painless rebirth
into a new body, fresh skin,

bladder, liver, kidney,
stronger bones, blood.

Aristaeus,
Grecian beekeeper,
believed honey bees
carried reborn souls.

Years later,
when the second swarm arrived
I knew he had returned to earth,
golden,
humming.

Light bulbs

MARIANNE BETTERLY

Five light bulbs
popped tonight.

The last time that happened
our house was filled with people,
air thick with grief,
the day after
Rick died.

Each time I said his name
lamps would flicker and dim,
fax machine fizzled,
phone battery died,
computer crashed,
my home blackened
without electricity.

I fumbled to find fuses
in the dark
without my husband.
He would have known
how to turn the lights on.

Maybe Rick wanted our house silent,
cut off from sound and light,
so I could feel him privately,
before returning to my routines
in a new world without him,
Maybe he was lingering in the dark,
a Buddhist soul waiting to be reborn,
or an angel, watching.

He had filled our house
with stage actor voice,
his laughter spilled onto the street,
spouting Elizabethan sonnets,
chanting Tibetan mantras,
telling me he loved me.

Now a shadow,
scent of Bel Ami cologne,
photo of a young man, smiling,
waving a ghost on a stick
in front of Winchester Mystery House,
a stack of fedoras,
a light that burnt out.

Sometimes I feel him late at night,
in a dream or
when a sound awakens me
in the hour of the wolf.

We are alone,
in altered states,
without baggage
of bodies.

I miss his touch.

Our son yells,
*Mom, we need to change
the light bulbs!*

Time to turn on
the lights.

None, I think

LISE MENN

This is a life different from anything I had imagined.
When the heater is not on, it is very quiet; I hear icicles melting in the sun.
You are not here, you will never be here again.
There is no point in waiting for you.
Soon, I will have your photograph enlarged and framed
So I can see your smile from across a room.

You are, of course, everywhere,
In this house full of our lives together,
But all thoughts of you are recollections.
There is nothing more to anticipate, no sound of our front door opening,
No ring of our telephone, nothing in our mail.
Which I have learned to call my door, my phone, my mail
Not even noticing that miser's singular.

I hoard you. I dive into my memories, I roll in them like Scrooge McDuck
        in his moneybin.
On lucky nights, I dream of you;
On the best nights, you are laughing and full of desire for me.

Everything about you is back, back, in some past, dreamed or remembered.
I live in a strange, quiet place where my heart beats slowly,
And I can hear icicles melting on a winter morning.

Alleyway

LISE MENN

I had forgotten about this little alley you used to
wait here with the car to pick me up after work I can
walk up it without crying because it's been four years now
but I can still see you sitting here
in the parked car.

And further up the alley behind a church, chords
on some organ and I think for the twentieth time or maybe the
            hundred and fortieth
Wouldn't it be nice to believe we will meet on any shore, beautiful or not,

Loving with Sinatra

CONNIE FISHER

Vanity-driven, I hadn't shed a tear for more than 25 years—my eyes would become too puffy. But when Russ, my husband of 39 years, died, at my pastor's urging I began to cry what seemingly became rivers, lakes and oceans. Realizing I need to contain the torrent, I began to gorge myself with tunes by Frank Sinatra. I'd play them all over the house and in the car, and sometimes they'd even put me to sleep. It worked.

I began to write about our life related to the Sinatra songs Russ and I loved. Early on in our courtship we'd hear "Come Fly with Me" and so we did, to the far reaches of the earth. Then in the end, at the crowded ICU unit of the hospital, Russ and I danced up to heaven as I bade him farewell. Approaching the Pearly Gates, I said, OK, St. Peter, hit it! "New York, New York"—and we twirled to that song with our usual abandon. Only this time he went on through the gates, while I remained behind.

I am prostrate, listening

ELIZABETH PAGE ROBERTS

I am prostrate, listening.
The flutter of a swallow's wings,
then a silence that deepens into the distance.
In heaving waves
renewed mourning crests
and empties out of me.
I senselessly wander behind the house,
a garter snake crossing my path
and into the english ivy.
I call my beloved,
certain as the wind picks up
that he answers me.
"I am here, all around you, inside your chest,
behind your eyes, in the moving currents of air
combing the trees.
Why do you always forget?"
I forget because I forget.
I forget because I remain hungry.
It's some kind of reflex.
I know.
I know.
There is richness and unity in me.
I'm not even close to alone
but all knowledge of the matter
seems to roll over me
like rain over oilskin.
I only crave the hands of the dead.
I crave them alive
dancing their certain language,
their speech of superlatives,
praising all.

I can only be healed
by the particular sweetness
of a man who saw into my soul
and climbed in anyway.
Emerson said "Give all to love"
and I reply, is there anything else one might do?

III
Coping (more or less)

My universe has changed

PHYLLIS WAX

and yet
the lake is no less green,
the blue of the clouded sky is no less vivid
The sun still shines
but the once exultant gulls
wail today

and the swoosh of the waves
is a leaky lung
steadily squeezing life away

No One Knows

ELIZABETH VON TRANSEHE

No one knows you're gone.
The police still want donations from you
And they summoned you for jury duty.
The Economist wants you to take advantage of an early renewal offer
And so does *National Geographic*.
An acquaintance asks how you are doing (I shake my head)
And a new friend wonders
About your picture on my phone.
They didn't know you.
Because if they did,
They would know
That it is a different world now.

How are you?

CHRISTINE SILVERSTEIN

Some time ago an old sage told me a secret. Never ask a child, "How are you?" I wondered the reason and he said, "A child does not think in these self-conscious terms. A child is not given to fits of introspection and self-analysis. A child simply is. A child is busy being." So, the sage told me, if you truly want to engage a child in a conversation, ask her, "What are you doing?" You will delight in her description of whatever the activity might be at that moment, and she will delight in the telling.

Today I am here to tell you a secret. Never ask a widow "How are you?" And if you wonder the reason, let the sage of my anguish and grieving tell you why. A widow does not think in the same language as she once may have. Her self has taken leave and been replaced by a powerful being. A widow is suddenly a being of introspection. A widow is not busy and so the ways of the world do not distract her, nor will she care to describe them to you.

A widow is not given to tidying up the truth. A widow is the truth manifest. So if you dare ask a widow "How are you?" be mindful that you will be seen by her subconscious and will be remembered by her heart in ways you never imagined.

I became very good at protecting all who would ask.
How are you?
I'm all right. I'm fine. I'm hanging in there. I'm feeling OK. Thanks for asking. I'm good. I'm doing well. I'm a little tired. I'm handling things. I'm fine, thanks to all of you. I'm getting better. I'm keeping busy. I'm making progress. Fine, better, well, good and thank you for asking.

If you have told these lies, which I am sure you have, over and over and over again, I know you. And if you have heard these lies and nodded with humble approval and felt set free by the relief they have given you, I know you too. Rest assured when you are tucking yourselves in at night that she is lying awake and you cannot hear her answers.

How are you?

I don't know. I am numb. I am filled with terror. I am a shadow now. I am lost. I am aching. I am nothing. I am, at this moment, no longer your daughter, your mother, your sister, your friend. I am no longer a lover.

How are you?

Please step back, you are standing on my guts which have just spilled onto the floor at my feet.

How are you?

I'm terrible. I'm not doing well. I think I'm going crazy. I have no desires. I can't see, hear, taste, or touch. I have no feelings. I am torn apart. I can't breathe. I am standing still while a tornado is ripping through my body tearing my blood vessels away from my organs.

How are you?

I am old. I am ugly. I am a monster inside a body that you once knew. I am exhausted.

How are you?

I am alone. I am afraid. I am filled with doubt. I am consumed by chaos. I am paralyzed.

I am humbled. I am repentant. I am living in a nightmare. Please shake me. Please wake me. Please hold me.

How are you?

I see you have two heads. I wish you really cared. If I tell you, will you run? How do you think I am? Please, take a crack at it. You tell me how I am. Can you believe you just ran into me? If only you had gone to the other market. If I tell you, what will you say? Will it be sympathetic? Will it be appropriate? Will it make it better? Here come those slings and arrows.

I know how you feel. I hope you're keeping busy. You look good. You will see the gift in this tragedy. Time will heal. The holidays will be tough. It will get easier. I'm glad to hear you're doing well. You're a strong person. Have you gone away at all? How are the kids? How's his mother doing? Call me if you need anything, anything at all.

How are you?

I'm shattered, thanks, how are you? I walk aimlessly through the rooms of my house, what have you been up to? I have woken up in the middle of the last 240 nights in a heart-pounding sweat, what's new with you? I sometimes wish I would never wake up, have you been on vacation this year? I ache for the arms of my sweetheart to hold me tight, how's your family? I feel barren and useless and creepy and mundane, seen any good movies lately? I'm terrified that I'll feel this way forever, I like that sweater you're wearing. I keep seeing his body on the hospital gurney, don't you love this weather. My broken heart is in my throat, let's do lunch. I'm so completely and utterly tired of being sad, thanks, how are you?

A widow is a special creature. She is part of an endangered species. She has a gift to share. She sees what you cannot. She feels what you have never imagined. She knows what you wish you could know but dread the wishing. So, the sage in me tells you, if you truly love the widow before you and you want to help her heal, say the following to her and listen with all your being to her answer.

I love you.
I want to know what you are going through, if not now, then some day I want to sit with you and hear it. My imagination is not big enough to comprehend the emotions you are having. How small and insignificant all of this worldly stuff must seem to you. Can you talk? You must miss him intensely. You must think about him in every moment. Which is harder for you, being alone or being in the world of people? Life must feel surreal to you. Do I have two heads?

I love you.
How many times have you been asked, "How are you" today? It's a dreadful question. It's an absurd question. Knowing you and seeing what has happened in your life makes me stop in my tracks and catch myself before I ask anyone that question again. How the hell can you answer that question in the aisle of a supermarket? Come back to the house, you say. Bring your toothbrush and call your boss. You will need a week to hear the complete answer. And you will never be the same if you listen. It's the question that the entire human race reduces itself to each and every day, in each and every encounter, and without the intention of ever truly hearing the answer.

I love you.
You are incredible. Even if you don't feel strong, I marvel at your strength. Look at you. How is it that you are still standing? What is keeping you going? I'm afraid to ask but I hope you can tell me. You loved him so deeply. It was obvious to everyone. You will love him forever. Can you talk? Which feels better, talking about him or keeping him to yourself? If you can talk about him, tell me about him. What made him so lovable? I don't care if you repeat

yourself. In fact, I pray that you repeat yourself so I can get it. I'm slow. I'm not in your world right now. I never knew him the way you did. I'm afraid I'll be jealous, but I really want to hear what made him so lovable. But only if you can talk. If you can't talk, would it be all right if I told you how I felt about him? If not now, then some day I want you to know how I felt about him and what he meant to me. Would you ever want to know? I am ready when you are.

I love you.

I'm probably going to fail you. My life is full of distractions and I need to live my life. You understand this about me and everyone else, more than I can ever imagine. We need to live our lives. And so I fear that I am not there for you. And my own guilt about that is hard to face. Being with you scares me and makes me uneasy. It's hard to be around truth manifest. I'm not strong enough to hear your truth, know what you know and try to give you what you need. If I tell you this fear, will you still love me? I just want to sit with you, walk with you, hear your voice, hold your hand, be in your home, look at your face, watch you pet the cat, and beg you to trust me.

Tell a widow that you have a feeling that time does not heal. Tell a widow that her man was a man among men. Tell a widow that what she is going through strikes terror into your heart. Tell a widow that you have much to learn from her if she ever feels ready to teach you. Tell a widow that you feel naked in her presence. Tell a widow that you hope she will tell you about how it was to love him and how it is to miss him. And, for your own sake, ask a widow for a hug. And when she wraps her arms around you, pay close attention to the love you will feel coming through her. If she cries, feel cleansed. Because it is love that heals.

Widow, Falling

PAMELA MANCHÉ PEARCE

Tell me how to live this beautiful life.
Tell me now.

Help me to make bracelets from tin cans
Christmas wrap from potatoes cut into stars and toilet paper
a gourmet meal from sautéed dice of pillowcase and
    hot rollers en brochette
to change my watch to an elastic bandage
to drive safely when I am blind
to know when I collapse, how to fall
to read the eyes of strangers when they ask me for change to get home
to ask strangers for change so I can get home,
in their eyes, and mine
to know when I am home and how to act when I am there.

Help me when I collapse.

The Machines

JACQUELINE KUDLER

First the grill ignition failed,
then, not ten days later and
two months after you died,
the fridge condenser went
but slowly—
for days I watched
the glacier crawling down
along the back wall.
It wasn't too much longer
before the timers in the double
oven and the upright freezer
quit, as if some universal
clock had simply stopped
somewhere, all dials fixed
at midnight.

By his fourth call,
the National Appliance guy
opined he'd never witnessed
such a run of luck—
everything breaking down
like that around me.
He hoped (with eyes
accustomed to assessing
hairline cracks and fissures)
that I was holding up OK.

I told him how my days,
amazingly enough, go well.
I wake, bathe, lunch with
friends, call the kids

and at night, when I sit
down at the table, I light
a candle at your place.
Oh, I'm doing well
enough, I said,
but given their histories,
the nature of their finely
wired dispositions,
I wouldn't presume
to speak
for the machines.

Managing

JACQUELINE KUDLER

December again and yes, I've managed
to muddle through 364 mornings
waking without you

> *we are on a boat again*
> *not a sailboat, but a tanker, or one of those*
> *destroyers from the mothball fleet*
> *and you're navigating the narrow catwalk*

waking each morning to the gape
of the day ahead, until the calendar clicks in,
propels me forward into what appears to be
my life

> *and you've fallen, fallen overboard*
> *stroking the tops of the swells below*
> *managing to keep even with the wake*

—managing to keep even with the machinery:
I've called your cousin Ruthie, smoothed down
your side of the bed each morning,
dead-bolted the doors each night and
edged the thermostat down toward
the glacial end of the gauge

> *I step away from the edge,*
> *begin careening down the catwalk*
> *into the cabin, calling all the time*
> *for help. . .for help*
> *the empty corridors call back and I'm running*
> *now past the engine room looking*
> *for the ship-to-shore console*
> *all along knowing I do not know*
> *the codes*

I do not know where you stashed
the camera or, for that matter, the paring knife

and the giant can of WD-40, but I've managed:
have hoisted sagging sliding doors back
onto their tracks, hammered the front deck
planter shut to keep it from leaking,
lived my way through your birthday,
our anniversary, and wrestled
the Thanksgiving turkey into
recognizable slices

> *and still you manage to stay above the waves,*
> *head down in the water, one arm then the other*
> *in that steady, unhurried stroke of yours*
> *as though you know, as always, exactly*
> *what to do to stay afloat in case*
> *someone can save you.*

Peninsula

DONNA HILBERT

Finger connected to the hand
by an isthmus of land.

I live on one,
travel to another to recover.

Yuke-a-tawn, Jack says, correcting my pronunciation.

At home, the bay on one side,
ocean on the other.

Here, it's ocean and sea.

Peninsula.   Might as well be an island
where I've washed up
salty, alone.

In Quintana Roo

DONNA HILBERT

Kathy gives me a card
with angels on dolphin back
swirling from sea to sky.

I think of the morning last spring
when from our window
we spotted a pod of dolphins
and you abandoned breakfast
to join them for a swim.

The card's inscription:
Together we will transcend
the illusion that is time
and space.

Transcend.   Joke on my license plate.
Comic motto for the nonbeliever.
Maybe where you are now
you know what that word means.

Not me.   I'm in Mexico.
Interregnum of old life and new.
Angry with you
for this dislocation.
I loved you in my other life.

I dreamt last night my friend
left her green parrot in my care,
but I failed to feed
or give it water
and when she came to claim it,

the bird lay dead
next to a vase of browning lilies.

Suddenly, you appear
in the dark sea
of my dream, saying
I don't remember when
we last made love.

Be patient, Dear Heart,
I'm learning how
to love you dead.

Dear one,

MAREAN JORDAN

Hours pass now—even days—when I don't think of you. The dog would not recognize your tread on the front steps. I sometimes fall asleep with the TV on, I've lost 20 pounds, I play your old guitar.

I stay up late most nights, and your side of the bed is piled with magazines, half-read books, pens and paper. I sometimes eat dinner standing at the kitchen counter, or in front of the refrigerator, almost never at our old table. I eat meat. I have a microwave.

You would be surprised by my garden, all root vegetables and greens in this stony soil, and on walks, wild flowers you would not recognize. The names of trails and lakes would be new names to you—Whychus Creek, the Metolius River, the Deschutes. Blue water gushing out of lava tubes, deep lava-rimmed canyons, the arid beauty on the east side of the Cascades.

I live at the foot of young mountains with deep roots. I live on rock, not along the tidal flux of bay and ocean, no longer in unstable earthquake country.

Now I pay the bills, wash the car, put on snow tires, have the oil changed, deal with a mouse in the pantry, the wasp's nest under the eaves. I have an electric drill, a toolbox, new neighbors.

No one in my life here knew you. No one understands that I was loved by someone as tall as you, someone other women wanted to go to bed with, someone who loved poetry and spoke eloquently and knew how to use tools. Your old students still get in touch, naming sorrows or triumphs they would have shared with you. When our son calls we talk twice as long, and half the conversation belongs to you, to the things that were unsaid between you.

I confess that the local library contains no book you would want to read, the newspaper contains no news, I no longer get the *Times.* Nothing happens here except small local sorrows and weather that would appall you—below zero sometimes, bitter wind blowing off the mountains.

The whirr and call of migrating geese, the shock of a star-heavy, moonless night sky, familiar scents carried by the wind. This is my life now, that I love, almost as much as I loved—and love—you, passionate, unknowable, and still as familiar and as present as my own breath.

Farewell to Sorrow

MAREAN JORDAN

Gray companion
loyal as a curse
you stand vigil at my bedside
or even, old familiar,
lie beside me
ashy head on the pillow
whispering.

Watcher in the dying light
you rustle your sad cloak
outside lit windows.

Singer of mournful arias
conductor of white-hot dreams
you offer me relics of the old life
a shaving brush
a sheaf of papers
a dry pen
empty shoes.

Sorrow, hear me now
I turn away from your chill comfort
your marble hand.

I choose another road
another loss
a different parting.

Widow's Lament

ROSALIND KALIDEN

I reject what society wants. *Stay alone, stay home and lick your wounds.* Stay alone! The sting! How ridiculous! The last thing I want to be perceived as is a recluse. And the second thing I want to avoid is spending the rest of my life with only other single women.

Why does my loss have to precede me into a room full of people? I am no less. I am *not* my loss. I refuse to give up my identity—the wholeness of me—because I lost my husband.

Other widows—I hate that word—may wallow in their grief. That's their choice. Not mine. And society be damned if everyone thinks they can pre-scribe how I should feel and act.

The loss of spouse is loss enough. But why do I have to give up my social life, my friends, my married friends! The shock of that!

What am I? The new leper? I walk into a room and the room clears or wives hook arms with their spouses! Come on! Lepers of old had to shout *Unclean! Unclean!* as they approached any people to warn them to clear out. As if *grief* were contagious, must I now shout out my widowhood in front of me before I pass, to warn those who don't want to *catch* it? Shout *Widow! Widow! Widow!*

What if I tell strangers, instead, that I am divorced, or never married or living with a significant other? These states have their own kinds of grief and stig-mas but not to the degree of the abandonment that is served up to the widow. Even widowers are treated more kindly. Hell, they're sought after!

Does Florida have to become my destiny? To walk among darkly wrinkled widows and widowers with the skins of barbecued chickens?

I grieve and maybe not grieve. Maybe I don't have the time or the luxury, to grieve. What do I grieve more? Missing my life's partner, my friend, yes, my soul mate? Or losing my social structure, my identity, my *who?*

I must sort through the true and the false friends now. I want to say to the world, *You idiots!*

In some way I am the aborted baby. My life has lost its social value! I want to say, *Wait, it's inevitable. You, too, will have your turn.* Or worse (maybe), *you'll die first.* My mother told me that she prayed to die before her husband. As she observed her many widowed friends, she decided that it was a punishment, a curse. *Then,* her remark baffled me.

Is recoupling better? Probably, but not that easy for strong women, for free thinkers. The whole new world of dating—I talk little then, listen to their cues or their silences, which tell me a lot of what I don't want to know.

How do you meet someone in your social strata? When they've dropped you like a hot potata?

The conundrum is that I have to be strong and many men don't like strong women! Not unless you're famous in your own right, like a Jackie Kennedy and a Mr. O, is there an exception.

Taking on the varied and sometimes serious problems of the divorced becomes *de rigueur.* The never married are a stranger lot. Their issues might be less apparent but are equally challenging and draining.

This is the age of frequent couplings and uncouplings. I'm not coupled. I'm a passenger car dropped off at the car barn lot and forgot. I'm an outdated airplane parked in the deserts of Arizona, my usefulness terminated.

How dare my *friends* tell me that they *feel sorry for me* or tell another it was a *severe blow,* or a *tragedy.* (It was simply a *death.*) They say *that* and still want to claim me as *friend?* I know, I know, they may mean well. Nonetheless, why can't we keep this simple? No additional dramatics needed. And for gosh sakes, let's not *play off* this!

I am invited to ladies' teas and holiday luncheons but not to dinner parties. Those invitations are reserved for their coupled friends and maybe widower friends with their new *honeys* or maybe for a specially selected single woman as an introduction to one of their carefully selected single male friends. A meddling of sorts? Or social engineering? The worse part is that they think I can't figure out what's going on. They think I don't know about it! I pray to God that I do not become that insensitive. I know, I know, I'm being *too* sensitive.

I do bless those who are kind enough to invite me to weddings and who include "and Guest" on the invitation. These *are* my friends. I am deeply grateful for the half dozen or so married women who will sacrifice weekend separation from their husbands to accompany me to a Sunday afternoon matinee at the theater. I kept my husband's season's subscription and invite these ladies as my guests. No, I do not expect them to, and they do not feel that they need to, reciprocate. I know that they are being extravagantly kind to me and I am eternally grateful.

Ultimately, though, it is loss, loss, and more loss. I suspect it will not end until I, too, am gone. Nonetheless, I elect *not* to remain silent about these things. I elect not to become the victim. I elect to remain proactive and maybe set an example for the thinking crowd, that widowhood is not a uniform social state and that I may even choose to make it different.

Now, let's see, I think I'll invite two or three of my favorite new couples, and a few interesting single men just to fill out the crowd, to my first dinner party as a single hostess. Care to join us?

Prayer Shawl

"ARIEL"

Worn carpet, smelling of
body sweat & animals.
Bright red shawl—soft soft yarn—
draped over bowed head;
this is a ritual since December.
Feet on carpet. Knees on raised stair.
Low tune from the heater as warm
current brushes thigh, back;
keeps cold from distracting.
Forehead resting on mattress,
palms clasp.
I do not pray for my sins;
       that would be dishonest.
I do not pray for your sins;
       that would be arrogant.
I pray for the courage of another day
       and the company of angels.

How I Carry You

"ARIEL"

At grief support, they gave me
a piece of petrified stone,
polished, to comfort me;
I wrote "adventure" on it, for that is how
I want to remember you—
or so I said.

But that stone speaks so much more to me;
when we would creek-walk
you would pick up stones, wet so they looked polished,
all their colors revealed,
mused as to their stories and how it ended up there.
Wood, rock. Water.
A palm-size fragment
shaped by nature.

This stone tells your story
though it never cradled in your hand;
it started as wood, malleable,
the sapling grew, a child of the earth
lived in forests—as you did when you ran
breathing scents of Douglas fir.
It was a companion of deer, of elk, of bear.
And when pressure came to bear down on it,
it became more stable, more solid
changing its substance but not its body;
its grain is still there
but it will not give way.
Then polished, all its color, its grain revealed
as if just picked up from the water.
Wood. Stone. Water:

transient into something almost eternal
that would endure.
I imagine that it is a fragment of you
nestled in my palm:

> That is how I remember you.

No Answer, No Message

CHARLOTTE COX

One of the hidden benefits you get,
losing your oldest pal, your lifelong chum,
is that now, at long last, at very least,
you have no one to answer to—

no mother peering into your school bag,
no father waiting up with furrowed scowl,
no spouse with probing pauses, sullen snits,
no kids with needs or wants or crazy fits—

really no one to question what you said or meant,
where you were, or what you did or didn't do,
what you were thinking, or not thinking,
how long you'll be, why you were short.

There's no call, no push, no pressing need
to answer all those pointless questions—
just the tangled darkness of your own thoughts,
the blinding light of truth inside your dreams.

In time you see there's no time left, no chance,
to answer what was once called for so urgently—
why you looked, why you didn't look,
why you cared, why you didn't care.

In truth, you don't care anymore because
there's all the time left in the world,
no one to answer to,
no one to call,
no question,
no answer,
no more.

Double Sinks

ROSELEE BLOOSTON

Every morning in our master bathroom I confront the fact that Jerry is gone. All I have to do is look at his sink: no toothpaste scum, no sprinkle of facial hair from his beard, goatee, or mustache. My husband couldn't make up his mind what look he wanted. The closer he got to returning to the Middle East, where he worked on and off during his last three and a half years, the more likely he would attempt to grow hair on his face. He had none on his chest, a characteristic he attributed to his Native American heritage. The absence of the tiny quarter inch shavings cuts to my core. We used to bicker over his messiness. I'd give anything to have the evidence of his living, breathing self spackling the basin next to mine. Instead, there is an empty bowl, pristine with disuse.

During the first few weeks after the funeral I would remove one object from his sink area every day: first the toothbrush, which I tossed, then the comb, and the soaps. I kept the old-fashioned shaving brush that he loved. I always enjoyed watching him lather his face with shaving soap from a wooden dish. It brought back the delight years before, of watching our toddler son gaze in awe at his father's mundane, manly ritual, and then sit on the closed toilet seat of our apartment bathroom, in serious grown-up mode while Jerry covered his smooth little face with cream and handed him an empty razor. The two of them would proceed to "shave" in slow, rhythmic strokes until all the white foam was gone.

I've tried to take over Jerry's side of the bathroom. I've filled his wicker container with nail polish remover, air freshener, and bath powder. I've stored toilet paper and tissue boxes in his cabinets. I've emptied his vanity drawers, thrown out prescriptions and extra razor blades, put the men's cologne's on my son's bathroom counter, keeping my favorite—the one that reminded me of his freshly shaved cheek—in the cabinet below my sink. I've only opened the bottle twice. The familiar scent is unbearable.

Every so often I actually use his sink to wash out my swimsuit or other delicates. But most of the time—unlike the bed, where I have gradually drifted center—in the bathroom, I stay on my side. After all, there's my sink the right one, and his sink, the left one, the one he left. The sink, the drawers, the surfaces where he so carelessly tossed his glasses or small change, remain bare, their clean emptiness the void that now is him.

Eleven Months

PATRICIA L. GOODMAN

Atop a hill
a whitetail doe
peers over tall grass,
snorts,
bounds off like a dolphin
across the field.
Fledgling martins
gather courage,
perched in nest holes
high above the pond.

The tiny wild thistle
has gone to seed.
Its silk flies
with a flick of my finger,
yet the leaden ache of you
is still so deep
I cannot reach it,
so tight
it binds my wings,

so blinding
I barely see
the myriad grasses
nod their graceful heads
as I walk by,
the bachelor's buttons
glowing lavender
in early morning light.

In the Woods

PATRICIA L. GOODMAN

Your pants are pressed
    and hung in your closet,
your shirts clean, ironed
    just as you like them.

Your glasses await you
    in my car,
your old brown jacket
    on its hook in the garage.

I haven't changed anything,
    except to sit at your desk
and begin to take
    into my own hands

the running of this farm;
    the bills, the mowing,
the tractor repairs
    you always handled.

In a disconnected way,
    I keep thinking
you might return,
    that this has been

a terrible dream,
    that I only imagine
I found you
    in the woods,

your new blue raincoat
    soaked and splattered
with blood.

Ties

SUSANNE BRAHAM

Hanging,
seven years
in my closet,
still arranged
by color,

paisley prints,
slanted stripes,
fleur de lis,
narrow to wide.

I folded each
into a box,
bubble-wrapped and
tissue-stuffed,
no space
for memories
to slide,

and dropped it
with a postal clerk
to travel
'cross the continent,

wondering if
our only son
would ever wear
the Thai tie,
its inky splotches
splayed like giant
jacaranda

on a bright,
orange background.

My closet wall,
now bare,
won't care
I've no one left
to dress
or dress for

Widow's Daughter

SUSANNE BRAHAM

She's come home
to live with me,
marking her space
with strands of
wild hair
and boots
left at the door
six days since the rain.

She must have been out
drinking last night.
This morning,
the front door was
neither locked
nor latched,
but I heard slamming
somewhere in the dawn.

Her father's books
grow dusty,
still shelved
along the walls
in an order
he alone had known,
worldly wisdom
languishing
between their
motley covers,

while fleeting time
proves sadly slow
to soothe
our weeping wounds.

Widowed, Turning Sixty

SUSANNE BRAHAM

I might remember to change my socks each day,
to comb my hair and maybe put on lipstick;
you wouldn't find the *Times* piled sky-high, half read,
if he were still here.

The fridge would be well stocked, with bagels, cream cheese.
Weekend brunches wouldn't go untouched, grow stale,
were my hungry guy around to remind me,
"Hey, it's time to eat!"

The children, still wanting his attention in
their grief, find in me at most a second best,
like most requests from charities he'd honored,
set aside with sighs.

The tempting ways I'd found to give him pleasure,
unrehearsed kisses, unexpected places.
Will there ever be another chance to love
as well as we did?

Way back when, heads turned as I'd go passing by—
construction workers whistling, ogling shapely
legs. No varicose veins to hide, I'd show my
mini-skirted pride.

How much easier to grow old with him home,
for though I try to fool myself, the mirror
shows it best when wrinkles on this aging face
force their way into

my consciousness. Now, talks we'd often had, of
moving on in days when one of us was gone,
creep ghoul-like back to haunt me in those cold hours
when sleep should have come.

A Christmas Trilogy

NANCY H. WOMACK

I

I am wearing your red jacket today,
the red fleece I ordered from L.L. Bean
two Christmases ago. It blends with the
fake poinsettias I brought for you. The
sky, an Ansel Adams photograph, as
gray as the granite vases in which I
anchor the flower stems, closes in,
anchoring me to this plot of dead grass.
Lingering in the cold, remembering
other holidays, I forgive you for the times
you wouldn't go with me to family dinners
because you didn't like crowds, the silly
games or the ostentatious prayers. I hope
you forgave me for going without you. At
least you were always there when I returned.
Now, on this red-gray day I leave you here
         to go home alone.

II

I forced myself to bake cookies this afternoon
not because I had a sudden urge for sweets
(God knows I've had enough already) but
because it is the day before Christmas Eve and
that is what I always do. Traditions must go on.
Tomorrow I will don your bright red jacket to
look as festive as I can, go visit friends and
         give the cookies away.

III

There are no Yule logs here, no carolers
out in the snow. There is no snow—just rain.
Il pleut—a phrase I learned in French class once
and thought it so beautiful I wrote a poem in
French with that title. My teacher said,
"That's nice." Nice? *Nice, Normandy,*
Paris! I'm going there this summer.
But this is now—Christmas 2006.
The gas logs are burning in the fireplace,
inviting and warm; the poinsettia Libby gave
me looks especially bright by the window.
Amid the Santa figures I've collected over
the years, I find a place on the hearth to have
fresh coffee from the beans Bill and Mary left
as a hostess gift; the book Angela sent is
poised on the table for an afternoon read.
There's dinner to make for tonight's guests
and gifts to put under the tree. I'll straighten
the house and put your red jacket away, but
not just yet. I want to savor the coffee a little
longer and dream of soft summer nights in France.
            Wild bells, ring out!
            It's Christmas day.

Curios

REGINA MURRAY BRAULT

The trailer-park widow tidies her lot,
dusts rootless roses that fade on her lawn.
She's like the bower bird tending her plot
listening to wind chimes from sunset to dawn.

The bird scatters stone, colorful feather
tempting her mate with bright pieces of hope.

The widow shuns chill, rose-fading weather,
Brown-study leaves on the metal roof's slope.
She scatters crumbs of stale conversation,
Carries her cobwebs away on her broom.

Bower bird preens her new generation.
Widow caresses a red plastic bloom.

Wind chimes are ringing, the autumn wind blows
tracks in the dust over feather and rose.

How to Get Around It

REGINA MURRAY BRAULT

Because you are too old to procreate
and too alone, ponder this;
if history repeats itself
you'll have three options:
become a stowaway
sneaking up the ramp
between fat-legged elephants
while praying they will march in unison,
or sign up for some snorkel lessons
then cling to the bottom of the hull
among the barnacles, and hang on,
or start hoarding scrap wood,
plastic jugs, anything that floats,
build a raft, and fend.
For if these waters rise again
where does it read there will be
room inside the ark for widows?

The Sisterhood

REGINA MURRAY BRAULT

Words travel fast on Widows' Row.
They say
another casserole to bake
another wake to walk through.

It is our rite
to pray for him who lies at rest
in his best suit—
something he would not allow himself
until today.

We'll drink a toast to him
who won't be home for her beef stew
although she'll set his place
and call his name.

We are the sisterhood of silence
who won't remind her
that we who must give life
are taught
to wear our emptied wombs
as though they were blue ribbons
from the county fair
and we who are dealt death
are taught
to plug our hollowed hearts
with homemade carrot cakes
while burying our men as we
do iris bulbs in gardens.

Instead
those of us who call it basic black
and crowd the back pews of the church
will watch and wait
while others tell her
time will heal all wounds

the words our tongues find hard to form

for each of us has learned
in turn
that there are secrets
widows keep.

Poem in Praise of My Husband (Portsmouth)

TAMMI J. TRUAX

(with acknowledgments to Diane di Prima)

I suppose it wasn't easy living with me either.
I mean back when you were — living.
You didn't know that I'd be a poet, and
I didn't know that you'd be dead.
And maybe that's why we did
cling to each other as if each thought
the other was the raft.

And now I, raftless, have been
treading water for years.
It's made me stronger than you'd
have ever thought I could be.
True, a few times, exhausted,
I've almost drowned, but
I always bob back up,
spitting and cursing,
the me you'd recognize.
And, yes, sometimes, I find
something to cling to briefly,
a bloated log that usually
turns out to be rotten on the inside.

But, sometimes, it's kind of nice,
floating freely, to new places
looking up at the stars
like those little kids
trusting the universe
about which I know nothing

and wondering if one of those
utterly unhelpful embers is,
as the Eskimos believe,
you.

Acceptance

TAMMI J. TRUAX

It was the first time
that I

fighting my way through
that crazy hazy cloud
between asleep and awake,

did not send you away
but let you stay
surrendering in peace,

closing my eyes
so as not to see
your invisibility,

and did not fear
that I could
feel you there,

like a real live man,
your arm draped across me
not frightening anymore,

as I finally decided
that I really don't mind
spooning with a ghost.

Gracie, Go Get Mommy's Glock...

TAMMI J. TRUAX

(with acknowledgment to Denise Levertov)

Yo Grief!
Get your nasty flea-bitten
gnarly old butt off my porch
before I fill it full
of the buckshot
you so richly deserve.
Don't think I won't,
I can you know.
I will too, you keep up
that lurking and circling
I'll shoot your miserable ass, and
don't think for one damn minute
that I'm gonna dig a hole
for you either,
I'll toss your mangy carcass
off the high-rise bridge
and leave you for the lobsters.
That would be righteous,
that would be just. In fact,
it's the best damn idea
I've had since you started hanging
around, but if you don't like it
you can tuck that tail
a little tighter
between your bitchy legs,
turn around, and save yourself.
Grief's not welcome here,
not anymore,
I'm done with ya.

Surviving with Gratitude

CHRISTINE THIELE

We are all survivors. Most of us have endured something difficult that we remember as something survived. Today is the anniversary of the hardest thing I've had to face. Five years ago today, my husband died.

I have this quote on my e-mail—nothing is more beautiful than the mantle of survivor—I love this quote. Today, I feel it more deeply than most days. Today though, five years down, I feel it differently. Today I don't want the only mantle I wear to be survivor. Today, I want my mantle to be as diversified as my soul. For many years now, all I have felt like is a survivor. I have felt my "widowness" to my core. Today, though, something feels different. I am not crying. I am not aching from missing my husband. Do I still miss him? Yes, very deeply…is there the physical pain and sadness as there has been in years past? Not today. Today I am more than survivor. I am Chris. I am no longer just widow, I am Chris with all that comes with that…mom, woman, single parent, cook, writer, lover of sunshine, dogs, and cool cars. Something is different today as I look at the landscape of my life that has been so changed by that day five years ago.

I have said this before, but not always meant it…I would do it all again even if I knew of the pain that I would have to endure…today, I can say it and mean it. That is a good day. I can recognize all the goodness that came from Dave and me knowing and loving each other. Again, it was never perfect, but it was ours. I am deeply grateful for knowing him, loving him, laughing with him, fighting with him, and building a family with him. I am deeply grateful today. I am even grateful for the pain of losing him. It has made me a better person…just as loving him made me better. Losing him has rocked me to my core, broken my spirit, left me lonely and broken and with all that, it has given me a great gift. It has helped me become more me than ever. It has helped me to know my depth, my capability, my weakness and my strength. More than anything it has let me know the capacity of my ability to love. To me, this is what really matters. I tell my children that we were created for really only one reason...to love. We are here on this planet to love each other, those who enter and exit our lives, and to love ourselves. Love has been a great gift in my life and in knowing and loving Dave, I experienced it deeply. In having our children and surviving his death, I have lived the words I tell my children. For when I was most broken, it was love that kept me going. It was the hope that love brings, even when the pain of love lost is so great that it hurts, that has filled my heart with gratitude today.

I can say with truth today: I am grateful. I am so grateful for knowing my husband and having him in my life that today I will celebrate. I will miss him forever; there is no changing that, but today I have been given the gift of a grateful heart, and I will be present to that feeling and share it with all those around me. So today, I am turning another page. I am moving from just a survivor back to Chris and all the gifts and garbage that entails. I will take survivor and weave it into all the other pieces of me. It will not be my mantle today, but be integrated into my being, into Chris. It will always be a large part of who I become, but it will not be how I define myself.

On My Own

THELMA ZIRKELBACH

On my own
I have had
A leaky roof,
A flooded bathroom,
A water heater leaking gas,
A crashed hard drive,
Thousands of dollars in medical bills,
A lawsuit over business assets,
Debts to you your friend refused to pay,
Squirrels in the attic,
A possum in the bathroom,
A broken nose,
A hysterectomy,
Carpal tunnel surgery,
Cataract surgery,
Vertigo,
And a hornet sting.

I've also had
A new car,
The garage restored,
The house repainted,
A garden planted,
Articles in anthologies,
A new book published,
A trip to France,
Visits to the Alhambra,
Troy, and Gallipoli,
My picture on a calendar
A blog with over fifty followers,
A date,

My hair grown longer,
My hair cut shorter,
And my seventy-fifth birthday.

There have been
Spring meadows sprinkled with bluebonnets,
Summer afternoons dazzled by heat,
Autumn doorbells rung by trick-or-treaters,
Winter twilights, hazy and dim—
And all without you.
Yet I still go on
And on.

Second Anniversary

GAIL BRAUNE COMORAT

Soon I'll start dating, maybe
a man whose heart has been slashed apart
like mine. I'll fall in love again. Marry

someone my daughter will never know.
Or worse: she will love him, too;
she'll ask him to walk her down the aisle,

and she'll forget her father's birthday,
his favorite song, how he played air drums
at stoplights, the way his moustache turned gold

in summer sun. Tonight we sit in silence,
friends and I, watch martins
slice evening light away. I'm voiceless—

tomorrow my daughter leaves.
I should have offered college nearby,
asked her to wait a year. Someone holds out

a fresh ruby-lit glass, my hand shakes
as I lift it to my lips. I turn away
to follow the martins as they sky-sweep,

wonder if they stop singing even briefly
when that last chick flees,
spreads wings toward the purple horizon.

The Widow Makes Pancakes

GAIL GILLILAND

I made pancakes this morning
First time since you died
And I sang "Nothin's gonna harm you"
From *Sweeney Todd.*
The pancakes were still raw inside
So now I know that what I saw
When you dropped dead in front of me a year ago
Was merely excellent sleight of hand,
The *legerdemain* of a great magic-man
The extent of whose talent we could not have known.

For here you stand now
As you did before
Shaking your head
Clucking your tongue
And saying your usual:
I told you so.

The Widow Decides to Get a Cat

GAIL GILLILAND

Make no mistake about grief.
It is what it is, it does what it does
And although it can't undo what is already done
Nor compensate for the sudden loss
It might make us kinder
More aware of the other guy's sorrow
More willing to address
Our most cherished faults.

So let us give thanks
For small comforts
Like the new cat, uncannily quiet
As she kneads & kneads against my lap
Then settles in the trough of my legs
In front of the fireplace, to watch.

Improbable Grace

CAROLYN STEPHENS

My old friend MM: We've known each other since we were both thirteen. We have a bit of a checkered history but were always friendly, except for that one night when he disappeared into the woods with my girlfriend at a middle school party. We lost touch after school, then I ran into him a few years ago (probably at the liquor store). He now has a property management/handy-man business. He likes it, because he's his own boss, and can arrange his schedule to get to all the games and performances of his three kids. We connected back up when Jeff was sick, when I hired him for some crappy little thankless task that Jeff and I could no longer do. I remember standing in the driveway that day, leaning against his dirty truck, and crying. He let me. He did not say it would be okay, because we both knew it would not be okay.

Never has he said any of the things a widow tires of hearing:
"How ARE you?"
"Let me know if there's anything I can do"
"Call if you need a hand."
or any inkling of
"So, are you seeing anyone yet?"

I hired him to plow my driveway while I was away for a week this Christmas. When I got home, after he had undercharged me for the job, he asked if I wanted him to keep on plowing for the winter. I told him I can't afford it. I can't afford to pay for things I can do myself. We have a giant snowblower; it takes an hour or two to do the job when it is working properly. It's not so bad.

But every storm since then, M. shows up in his big truck, plows the driveway clear in two minutes, and disappears into the dark. If I say, "Send me a bill, dude," he laughs, waves, drives away on his appointed rounds.

He would be so embarrassed to hear that he is the definition of grace in my life. Most of his friends would be shocked. He is not an obvious example of a good Samaritan. He drinks far too much. Is way overweight. Does as little work as possible. Is not opposed to being paid in cash. Is divorced; he and his ex-wife have nothing good to say about their erstwhile quarter-century marriage. I am sure he tells no one of his repeated good deeds to the widder woman.

He just does it. Then goes home and pops open a cold one.

Still Life

KATHERINE J. WILLIAMS

Most mornings, I do not see the pillow
still fresh from yesterday's making.
On a night when the air is a thicket
of heat, I search for the cool pool
of sheet on the other side of the bed.
In this new economy the currency
is initiative. I set the table for seven,
specialize in the anthropology of three.
I'm an accidental citizen of a country
where things stay put; where I sleep
when tired. In the old dispensation,
travel meant time to be a tourist
in each other's bodies, foreign land
as background. Now, I practice
being a lover to the world, tracing
the shoulders of a new city, tasting
its breath. But tonight, my houseguest
calls his wife—*late, laundry, tarmac*—
the words like the cups and petals
in a Zurbaran painting,
intimate reminders
of a larger fleeting life.

Resurrection

KATHERINE J. WILLIAMS

After reading a Dharma talk by Richard Baker Roshi

I look up *inosculate,* the word clunky
on the tongue, like something unchewable.
How can this mean *to unite intimately?* I think
of my husband's ashes under toppled headstones
on a hillock in Vermont and somehow flip
to *resurrection,* but *rising of the dead at the last
Day of Judgment* is not what I'm looking for.
Closer might be *resurrection fern—a drought resistant
evergreen that appears to be a ball of coiled,
dead leaves but revives, with moisture.*

Back then, I peppered the world with obituaries
and death notices, watching his name drop off
sale flyers and water bills. The fraternity
magazine he never read hung on the longest,
like an ancient mariner compelled to tell
its tale even though no one was listening.
A Value Village truck consumed the clothes
in which he knew me. I found a new address.

Yet recently, thanks are sent to Charles and Katherine
for contributions made in my name only. Letters
begin arriving addressed to him. In the mail today,
a postcard from Gilbert School, requesting news.
I dial, inform the woman that my husband has been dead
for 14 years. I hear her breathe, type, then state,
"I have entered that he is currently deceased."
I say, "Yes. Currently. But if that changes,
I'll let you know."

Irradiation

ANN CEFOLA

What is the half-life of grief? 325,000 years and waste
that must be encased in glass. It is, as Mme Curie coined, *radioactive,*
the mean free path to a new self unwanted and unasked for.
In the bereavement group, they say, *You seem to be doing better.*
I shrug. Run a hand through my hair. The counselor says,
Grief is a river. You must get in the middle of it.
Loss a green glow, like blue rods in boric acid, $E \neq mc^2$. Time stops,
matter doesn't equal energy, everything matters and nothing.
Symptoms: vertigo, cuts, broken bones, and the call to eat every pill
in the medicine cabinet. But we keep returning to the funeral home to talk,
where pallbearers in blazers joke. They above all know the cure, and we wait
for it, a way to live with exposure, a way to rinse off the bright blue cobalt
that lines the psyche, this new element in our periodic table.
O Plutonium! Named after the farthest planet, you know what it is like
to emerge from a chemical chain reaction.

What Yields to Winter

ANN CEFOLA

Soft earth, soft hayed earth,
last pumpkins dotting the straw field,
dead mouse-dirt road.

Pale butternut coins
shivering like parchment. Leaves,
tossed and crumpled, each one, as if by hand.

Saying *poplar* or *white pine,*
the tree man needs to cut wood from wire.

And what refuses:

Ancient pines, like stallions roaring on a rope,
against iced wind. Snow
like last ghostly moths of summer.

Lone birch a chalk mark. Four poplar branches
suggesting everything has a frame.

I enter my yard as a scythe, O birch; I repeat *poplar, white pine,*
and the cutter pats their bark, tenderness for what he must take.

Sorrow what overtakes me: Elegant silk pulley, birch looks to open sky.
Nevertheless you must stretch toward it, she says. *Try.*

Widow's Weeds

JOANNE SELTZER

The time of mourning past
she casts aside invisible
widow's weeds washed in tears,
changes to pants, shirt, and shoes
fit only for yard work.

Periwinkle brought from another house,
a different State, a distant life
grow luxuriant under pines.
Widow plucks, digs, cuts
native and alien species.

Here a white worm. There a butterfly.
Wild strawberry seeded by birds.
A toad. A dragonfly. A honeybee.
Two kinds of ferns, unwelcome beauties,
near impossible to uproot.

Where pines and periwinkle end
semi-tall grasses bloom as if
the sun will never die. Like birds
children pushed gently from the nest
cultivate lives of their own.

Sleep

JOAN MICHELSON

We were young. No one bothered
much with clothes. You tried a few
other girls before we met
but none passed the test you set:
what mattered was how you slept.

With me, you professed to rest.
So the marriage we grew into
which failed so many other tests
and tested us until the last
lasted until death.

And now undressed and wrapped in sheets,
I move from bed to bed to couch
as if reproached by sleep itself.
I lie awake and watch the dark.
I watch a thousand things unseen.

And when the cat returns at dawn
and he curls up, I think of us
as once we slept. Then I could rest.

Scar

JOAN MICHELSON

They say I fell because you fell.
First day back at work, I missed the kerb,
landed on my face, broke my glasses,
and gashed my cheek and lip. I was taken

straight to A & E. Then there I sat
filling in the form for your bronze plaque
with words that Jess and I agreed were fit:
Father Lifemate Teacher Poet.

I totalled up the cost, wrote a cheque,
had time to find a hot drinks machine,
and to doze. The wound, with grit inside,
had time to close. When the doctor looked,

he took in breath. He'd have to open it
to pick out dirt, clean, then stitch. This wouldn't
be pleasant. For me, no matter. Since you'd been gone,
my body had felt distanced beyond feeling.

Now I have a scar from cheek to lip,
a secret Braille that my fingers read.
And when I rest my face against your plaque,
the thin ridged mark like the stigmata burns.

Message to Satan

JOAN MICHELSON

Seven times in seven years, I've written
a reply to you and hit 'delete.'

Am I angry still? Still baffled?
Why did you speak for Geoffrey his last night?

I'd like to shake you, Satan, until your bones
are fit for nothing but an iron stockpot.

Go on gloating. Clerks like me and my dead
husband helplessly obey an urge

to write. Everything goes down on paper,
or into the computer. We file, read, rewrite.

Again I read your letter. I want an answer.
Must I accept no answer? Your phone

does not connect. It's my receiver I hear
humming crassly. I watch it hit the bed.

Betrayals

KRISTINE SHOREY

One

December 1988. It's Christmas time, a few weeks after my husband's death, and I'm still on bereavement leave. My boss comes to my house, bringing me a tree ornament wrapped in a box. It is a large silver ball with a Mickey Mouse. When I hang it on the tree I notice it has a year printed on it as well—from a few years back.

My boss is a few years older than I am. He is single, slight, a couple of inches taller than my 5'4", his face deeply pockmarked, his nose too large for his thin face. He wears unfashionable wire-framed glasses, speaks in a working-class Boston accent. Our group has nicknamed him the Chihuahua. I have never thought of him as anything but a boss. During this visit he exhibits a shy awkwardness at odds with the brisk, confident businessperson I know him to be. He is wearing a soft sweater; until now I have only seen him in a suit. His voice is uncharacteristically gentle. He bends his head toward mine so we are in a sort of huddle, looking toward the ground.

"Are you, um, are you (pause) seeing anyone?" he asks.
My image of him, already shifting, now flips entirely. My heartbeat quickens just as it used to when I was single and could tell a boy was going to ask me out.
"No," I say. I lift my eyes to meet his. He isn't looking at me.
"If you decide to, I can ask HR about getting you some names."

My face freezes. He is asking me about a THERAPIST. *My husband has been dying for two years and you wonder if I have a THERAPIST?* I want to shout. *How stupid can you be?* My anger is at my vulnerability, but I can't see that yet.

Two

February 1990. It is a relief when I'm recruited for a job in another part of the state. I'm ready to leave my job, the company, the region. When I first returned to work I felt like I was wearing a sign, "My husband just died." People either avoided looking at me, or would ask me "How *are* you?" in a way that I never knew how to answer. When I started dating a recent widower, I felt that sign had turned into a scarlet letter.

I am at an interview lunch with my potential boss. I really want this job. She's taken me to a trendy white-tablecloth bistro. I am wearing a suit that seemed more chic in the store. She is wearing spike heels, a tight skirt, a silk blouse, and heavy gold chains around her neck. Her hair is sprayed in place, her makeup elaborate and perfect. Her long red nails tap against my résumé, which she has laid on the table. She points to the address line.
"You live in a house?"
"Yes."
"Are you married?"
This throws me. I don't want to lie, but I don't want to go down Widow Road, either.
"Not anymore." I keep my game face and hope she won't probe for details.
"But you got the house. Good for you." She smiles and nods. Not correcting her impression just about kills me.

Three
September 1991. The wedding planner is showing me and my fiancé the playlist for the band that we've hired. We're selecting a song for our first dance. They don't play "our song"—"Baby, I'm Amazed," by Paul McCartney.

"Let's go with this one," my fiancé says, pointing on the playlist to a Linda Ronstadt song.

She hands us the sheet music. I read the lyrics, "I've been waiting all my life for you, and now you're here." He starts to hum it. The song has been played often on the radio recently. I like it but am surprised at his choice. Doesn't he get how inappropriate it is for two people who have each been happily married before? *I must be making a big deal out of nothing,* I tell myself. I don't want to argue.

"Sure, that's fine," I hear myself saying.

When we dance to the song at our wedding, I shrink inside. I would give anything to change it. But it's too late now.

Guilt

SEREN FARGO

A crime has been committed.
A morbidity as I prepare my dinner with pots and
utensils that should not belong to me.

The guilt weighs heavy in my gut, as
I fill your tupperware with a salad for work, and
remember the pallor of your skin that I too quickly
dismissed.
As I put away your heavy pot I used for making
not-nearly-as-good-as-yours popcorn, and hear the echoes
of your unsatisfied complaints
of fatigue.

In an attempt to soothe myself, I put ice cream
in my mouth with the fancy spoon you used to own, and I
remember
your last night on earth,
troubled expression, and my walls of disconnect.

With my mouth full of creamy
coldness and your hard metal spoon in my hand,
I find myself feeling like a child with puffy cheeks, trying
to hide the crumbs on her face; or a teen
with pockets full of items that were never paid for.

And then I recall the occasional news story
of the killer who ate food from the refrigerator
before leaving his victim's house.

Unpalatable

SEREN FARGO

Living with grief is like having to eat what is put in front
of you.
You look for the napkin,
          or the dog,
but they are nowhere in sight. So you have to swallow the
whole thing.

The friends who are willing to sit at the table with you
are the water that helps wash it down.

To a husband, saved by death at 48

"M"

You will not see me, now
older than you are.
You will not watch my toenails
harden into turtle shells.
You will not complain about my face
creams costing more than most people
spend on groceries in a month.
Nor see me apply them to my hands
because no matter how young a woman's face looks,
it's always the back of her hands
that give her away.
You will never think of me as a suitable gift
for a toddler on Christmas,
shrunken to doll size, wrapped in skin
as thin as bargain paper. You will not be the one
to drive me home wet
from the Lloyd Center Mall
where restrooms are hidden away like exclusive resorts
down remote corridors.
You will not need to remind me
to take my umbrella when it's raining,
nor find my car keys
in the refrigerator next to the eggs I bought yesterday
and we will not laugh about it.
You will not hear me struggling with nouns.
You will never be awakened late on Friday evening
by a ringing phone, wife gone from your bed,
Detective Copeland saying she was found asking people
to help her find her husband
at a Taco Bell on Burnside
that stays open from 5:00 a.m. to 5:00 a.m.

every day but Sunday.
Someone else will sit with me in the ER on New Year's Eve
listening to an alcohol-poisoned teenage boy
vomit in the next room while we wait for news
about the golf ball on my temple, received for nothing more complicated
than slipping off a curb.
You will not see me without my teeth
or my gallbladder.
Never need to learn I've been sexually inappropriate with Paul
in The Pearl Memory Care Residence at Kruse Way
where I live apart from you for the first time in fifty years.
You will not be the one to close my eyes.

Salt

"M"

In this room down a hall
at the Hopewell House
every Wednesday
from 6:30 to 8:00 p.m.,
the widowed have agreed to meet
to lick the salt block.
My name tag reads
Albino deer (recessive rarity): widow at 35.
Dun-colored Helen and Marie
mistake me for a sheep or a goat
as we draw our chairs into a circle
of circumstance. Muscles in their aged faces
twitch with the greed of suspicion.
In the larger world,
Jean and I would sit in adjoining streetcar seats,
read our newspapers,
and never share a headline.
Even Doris, who drags the remains
of a personal god at the bottom of her purse,
tucked next to nonprescription reading glasses
she bought on sale at Walmart,
shrinks from my pink eyes.
Louise has ten grandchildren,
three she and Harry were raising
because her daughter is, well, you know,
she doesn't want to say. She won't tell you either
that when Harry up and died like that,
some small part of her wished
he'd had the decency to take those kids with him,
but he never even took them to the park.
Betty lost a husband and found

a lump. Elsie says when the ambulance comes
to the Ridgewood Nursing Home,
they don't turn on the sirens
for fear they'll incite a riot
of dying. Ida says yeah, she knows.
She's lost two of them that way. I nod.
Judith's raised eyebrow asks
What could one with hooves so pale know of loss?
A marriage must be long
to be 40-years deep,
and grief is a black market business
best kept to themselves. If I taste it,
others will want it.
Young bucks will be dying in droves.
In war, in the streets,
in flaming buildings.
Or quietly in a bed next to me at night.
That sting in the wound, that particular tang
on the tongue, are theirs.

Keep me away from the salt.
Their old ones are sanctified,
their sorrow is sacred,
denial alive in the hide.

Fresco alfresco

"M"

Francesca wants to know *who do you think*
you are, Michelangelo? Contentment is lying
on the scaffold with dye in its eye.
I've gone unwashed for so long, I offend
myself. Concern wets the family's hair
like holy water. *When will it be done?*
they ask of a composition with no prelude,
no mezzo, no denouement. I eat from tubes
of cadmium red and they shit scarlet
saints. Nudes in the papal chapel scream
Lasciami stare when Braghettone
gives them pants. Simon laughs at everyone
who carries someone else's cross. *Don't you know*
Chi s'aiuta Dio l'aiuta? Go get your own
grief, don't help yourself to mine. People are selling
it at the cemeteries in different denominations.
The widow at a grave in Buccheri buys
a year's worth. Her relatives should give her
at least that long before they shove
a ticket to America in her hands.

I could be your change of scenery, says the man
across the table in Gino's Pizzeria on 5th.
His name is Jacopo, the nephew
of Uncle Sallie's friend. The lowest leaf
on the rose in the bud vase starts to burn
when he lights the votive candle
like he does every Sunday at St. Anthony's
to pray for an end to his mother's
fascio di nervi, to say nothing of his own.
I blow it out. He wears failure

like plaid pants with a striped shirt and winks
at me like he has something in his eye.

Author's Notes:
Lasciami stare: Leave me alone; go away.
Chi s'aiuta Dio l'aiuta: God helps those who help themselves.
fascio di nervi: bundle of nerves.

She Considers Widowhood

NATASHA SAJÉ

in the same way she's always prepared
herself—a book for the long
wait, chestnut flour for the cake
she'll make when it's cold again.
Maybe she'll lose weight, like her mother,
having no one to eat with,
and finds it odd to think this,
but she can't help the dog of her consciousness
racing ahead and then back to her side.
So much for *be here now.*
What will she do when a pipe breaks
or the cat brings in a live
bird. Her heart pounds.
She'll call someone, she tells herself,
that's all. The habit of thinking ahead is not
seemly now, she knows,
as it signals an ability
to go on without the one she loves best
and it prefigures readiness
like a closet full of canned goods.
She avoids a metaphor for love
in the same way that she avoids thinking
about other aspects of the future but she feels guilty
for spending energy thinking at all.
She should be channeling brainwaves to make him well
or just looking into his eyes.
If he dies she'll surely regret
not having spent every possible minute with him.
Married to the idea of being half
of a pair, after thirty years, reading
each other's minds, feelings emanating

like sound waves, what would it be like
to lose that. How much she's learned through love
about *everything,* including that quadrant of self
visible only to others but exceptionally
accessed through the one who knows her best.
She considers that square closed to her.
Maybe she'll get rid of the television.
Maybe she'll move.

Persevere and Endure

CHRISTINE THIELE

per-se-vere—To persist in a purpose, an idea, or a task in the face of obstacles or discouragement.
en-dure—1. To carry on through despite hardships, undergo. 2. To bear with tolerance: endure the consequences.

To persevere and endure are two concepts that are a big part of my life since my husband's death. It is really the only way I know how to exist anymore. Days are not the way they were when he was alive. There is a joy lacking in my daily existence. People around me may say that is my responsibility to find that joy again. The way I see it is different, I think. For every day I make it through, I find victory. I have endured another day. I have persevered and taken another step toward my continued healing. My loss is so enormous to me! Not everyone sees it that way. Many think I should move on (whatever that means?), but I'm pretty happy to be able to endure day to day. Life is empty without my husband. I go through the motions of day-to-day life, but I still miss him, his support, his humor, his smile, and so many more things every day.

Each day for me is filled with things that I used to look forward to in the morning. Now they feel empty and stressful. Handling my life by myself is sad for me. I liked being part of a team. I liked having someone else to share my day with every night. I liked having someone to joke around with—who actually thought I was funny—my kids totally don't get me! A day shared with my husband was a day worth sharing for me. Now, I am sad that he is not here to joke around and share my day with every night.

I have friends and family, but let's face it, they have their own lives—they have their own family and people to share their day with every night... sometimes there is just not room in their lives for me...and that is fine...but for me it is something I endure.

I endure waking up alone in the quiet morning. I persevere when financial and work stress is mine alone to handle. I endure when my children fight with each other and think I'm a bad mom for not letting them have that sweet treat before dinner. I persevere when my car breaks, my sinks leak, or there are just too many tasks for one grown-up to handle. I endure when I get into bed alone at the end of an exhausting day.

This is my life for now—persevering and enduring—until it passes and becomes something new and more hopeful. I endure. I hope for joy to return and recapture a time when I feel loved again. I look to and hope for a time when days will be less of something to endure and become something to enjoy and share.

Something Someone Said

ANDREA S. GEREIGHTY

Chocolates hang red
gold foil hearts on the tree
three women speak at dusk.

Ushers in tuxedos
fuss with parishioners' tickets
we glide past nods into the
poinsettia incense
baroque choir subverts space
light fills the eschatological silence
Outside in the cantaloupe sky, faces
of houses waken as porch lights click
in that moment at dusk when it's
three shades lighter than gun-metal grey
peace can turn melancholy if thoughts are
not exercised carefully, the way a runner
would stretch out before a race.
Train daily; idleness makes
7 pm a vulnerable hour.

Watch for it, that bad section of road in your mind
jagged in the unfamiliar fading light
glance at your watch; doorknobs come and go
minutes move you through two hours
9 pm eases tension: write, read, take a bath.

The night from this side of the city
resembles Manhattan: subways, lights, taxis,
people; Broadway, not St. Charles Avenue.

Shoes

HOLLY ZEEB

I'm tying the mates together,
each to each: piles of sneakers,
work boots, ski boots,
loafers—all run-down, wrinkled
with wear. I heave
two lumpy bags into the trunk
for the Salvation Army.
A furtive mission,
this disposal of effects.
Hunching over, eyes averted
as if I'm guilty of something,
I hear you protest—*Wait!*
I might need those again.
Weeks ago you were eager,
wondering what you'd do with
the next ten years of your life.
How did your steps
veer into this mystery?
I call after you
with poems, until
they, too, disappear
on their stumbling feet.

Exterminator

HOLLY ZEEB

He came in his white hazmat suit, veil
    like a halo, spray gun in hand.
        You wouldn't have believed

the carpenter ants, wasps,
    meal moths swarming
        biblically that day.

You, gone ten months, yet they were abundant
    and intent on their business.
        He fingered the dust,

inspecting for ant parts, recommended
    the four-fifty treatment. Set out
        a seductive pheromone trap

for the moths in the hall, doused
    the wasps in their secret hole
        In the garden. They furied up

around him, but he was young, immune—
    wrapped in his white cotton clothes
        like an angel,

as if he could protect me. A hit man
    claiming to love his work,
        as if he knew everything of death.

Camp Numbers

BARBARA BALD

I've been in these woods seven days,
fed our fish twelve shrimp pellets,
filled two hummingbird feeders with red juice,
given our cat ten doses of pink medicine.

I've live-trapped twenty-eight field mice
with the Tin Cat trap you bought,
rescued our Brittany's toy four times from the river,
seen one person, the gas man fixing the fridge, in two days.

I've written thirteen poems,
five about your untimely death,
cleaned six cabinets to rid rodent remnants,
replaced one roll of toilet paper in the outhouse.

I am still waiting for one of you.

If I Write Enough

CARY FELLMAN

words spilled onto paper
will wash away the anguish
clutching my throat
maybe then
my sorrow will be released
and pain will leave my belly
the grief squeezing my heart
will loosen its grip

maybe
if I spew out despair through my pen
shattered dreams will be swept away
replaced by something   anything

then my eyes
won't see through a film of tears
and the empty space inside
can be filled
with God's
healing grace

What will there be

ELIZABETH PAGE ROBERTS

What will there be
if not poetry in the morning?
Will there be trees, like poems,
succinctly beautiful,
open to interpretation,
read for their wisdom,
read to wash us clean?

What will there be
without these questions
each new, open day?
Will the patterned chaos of shadows
on the sun-soaked snow offer a place to wonder?

My clouds seem so petty,
as the lush ones above move
like great white dragons
against the cornflower-blue depths of sky.

Some russet leaves still hopelessly cling
to these abandoned trees.
We must be like them,
forgetting when a thing is done.
When living is done for this one life
or that one.

We cling to memory like branches
as though some thread
to resurrection exists.
And yet it is simple,
Nature's inexorable dance.

We must float downward
from our hold on some hopes
and quietly nurture the ground
for different growth.

widow, anew

ELIZABETH PAGE ROBERTS

i have given away
the fear of fear
left strewn across
the wooden floor planks
of your room
ancient questions
outgrown musings
of emptiness
and futile wishing

i have molted
leaving behind
a tough if iridescent shell
once insistently
made of strength
for the sake of strength

now my nakedness
shifts into an open light
onto a steady path
a broad levity
a precious range of ready

now my strength
is the letting go
the falling
the grieving
of grief's departure

hints of life
in these hard fierce bones

now strength
is coiled in memory
and propelled
by a remade heart

Why I Paint

DONNA WAIDTLOW

Another autumn painting
Big splashy globs
Of yellow and orange oils
Mimic dying leaves
Streaks of topaz and rust
Mimic dying grass
No one says, *You're still obsessed*
With his death!
No one puts their arm around my shoulders
Says, *Get over it! Get a life!*
No one reminds me that we fought like banshees

There are no questions where I have no answers

I mix the crisp blue
Of a cooling sky
The tinge of absent breath
But no one knows that the purple
Is my bruised heart

Sounds sentimental
When I say it straight out
Doesn't it?
But I can hide in the trees
Linger in grief's embrace
No one knows I'm here

If they notice anything
It will be my brushstrokes
My lack of perspective

The Farmer's Widow Gives Him
a Piece of Her Mind

MAUREEN TOLMAN FLANNERY

Everything else seems to be having life
and having it damn abundantly
if you ask me.

A new cottonwood shoot,
its sights on a slice of sky,
aims to tower high over the house
with roots scooping up the foundation.
It's taking full advantage
of the neglect provided
by my trying on life-without-you for size.
This life is, by the way, way too big
and hangs on my sunken chest
like a hand-me-down housedress.

The bankers have been by twice
to find out why you had the cheek
to die at the peak of growing season
and to acquaint me
with the red-ledger fruits
of my current failure to function.

This damn Queen Anne's lace,
light and airy as it is, springs up at will
as if the home place were an open field.
And your fields,
my sweet weed-attacking dear,
your fields are looking as scruffy as I feel
and I fear, come harvest season,
I won't care enough to get out of bed.

After Her Death

MARY OLIVER

I am trying to find the lesson
for tomorrow. Matthew something.
Which lectionary? I have not
forgotten the Way, but, a little,
the way to the Way. The trees keep whispering
peace, peace, and the birds
in the shallows are full of the
bodies of small fish and are
content. They open their wings
so easily, and fly. So. It is still
possible.

       I open the book
which the strange, difficult, beautiful church
has given me. To Matthew. Anywhere.

What the Widow Learns, 2

HELEN RUGGIERI

the remote is all yours
you never have to watch another hockey game

you get to choose which side of the bed
you want to sleep on, close to the clock, the phone

all the drawers are yours
all the closet space

you cook what you want
when you want it

you make all the things he hated
the way you like them

the car is always there
you always fill the tank

you rearrange the room
move the tattered Lazyboy

no one yells because you've
left a tool out of its place

and finally the empty place
he left fills up

and only on snowy mornings
does the unshoveled walk
give you away

323 West 22nd Street

ELLEN PECKHAM

And so I sold it—the previously unappreciated wreck
           of 1835.
Sold the fireplaces and moldings, the crooked steps,
the fig tree and fishpond as wide as his circled arms and his
           elbow-deep,
the ghosts, the too-dry planks, the low cellar arches, the studio
           on the roof added in 1926;

sold all we had loved and repaired and polished and celebrated.
For each time I left him there in his hospital bed I died a little
           death, not at all
sensual as the post-coital: a slow death coming toward us
loss by loss—lost speech, lost memory, lost recognition.
           No regeneration possible.

How could I live among the tiles and shelves, iron stairs
           to the garden,
cook in our kitchen, sleep in our bedroom? All the objects
which once surrounded him, though inert, yet mourned,
           draping me in shredded veils:
pain, such pain, after each visit disemboweling.

And so I sold it, emptied it with grief and vengeance.
           Once almost
burned it to the ground lighting a fire of gleanings from our
           Shelter Island beach walks.
Visited pretending cheer, gave hugs that could not be returned,
           pretend "dates" at the cafeteria
and, coming home, cried and drank, raged and cowered.
           Then went back.

And so I sold it—our palace, our creation, our center of peace.
How could I maintain a garden where so much salt fell,
                    fertilize what lives as you do not?
Our little deaths grow 'round compressing our flesh,
                    decompose it, preparing us.
There are no first acts now, no catalyst for drama, denouement,
                    only curtains, curtains.

So after all of this how could I, how could I,
                how could I
leave you to the needles and tubes, the kind people
                    with no sense of you,
who never knew your intellect, humor, musicianship, heroism
                    (only told to me by others)?
And keep coming home which was no home

without you and not moved, not sold?

Grief

IRIS LITT

I buried grief without a ceremony
accelerated past the cemetery
tossed grief out and drove
over the speed limit
directly to a party

but your ghost
in protest
went with me.

The dead, the garbage and the rage

IRIS LITT

Kilroylike I peer a little way beyond
the litterbugged ditch of the dead, the garbage and the rage
to the potential peace of Saturdays with poems
the pleasant moment of this you at the door
or you other laughing in the café.
People don't kill themselves because they
don't want their lives
but because they want something their lives won't give them
but don't believe they have a right to fight for.
Now my-dear-all-those-years-behind,
I've had to walk that same terrain
to know why you did it.
Well, the earth is strewn with bodies. One is you.
I will live to cook a good stew,
talk to my children, finish these poems,
make love to a few special people, know possible peace.
Tastes of happiness tease me back.
I'm sorry you stopped short, dropped back, couldn't hold.
I forgive you and I'm sorry, sorry, but I grow old,
have to leave you behind,
behind with the blind
anger, guilt, and pain
and try again.
That half a loaf we joked about:
I'll take it.
I'd like to join you
but I'm sorry, sorry, sorry I can't make it.

Death of a friend

IRIS LITT

My mother said
that when I was small
I would look at my cereal
then called porridge
and say All Gone

and when my two-year-old
who didn't know the word
for death
asked where Daddy was
I said All Gone
and heard
his sad small voice:
Daddy All Gone.

Well, now they're all All Gone
some going fast
some going slow
but all going going going
going going Gone

and there is nothing to say
except that this
is a day of golden sun
and flawless sky
and I've got it
to take or to leave.

Do It Yourself

LISE MENN

Some things you have to do for yourself if you want them done right.
Ironing your favorite dress with the tricky collar,
Making hot chocolate the way you like it.
Feeling sorry for you.
Nobody else can do it properly.

Feel sorry for yourself.
Having lived in paradise for however many years,
And now finding yourself like the rest of them, the singles
Whom you felt smugly sorry for (and how much good do you think that
      did them?)
Now you too have aborted flirtations with men who were hopeless to
      begin with,
Lapses of judgment in attempting lesbian advances,
Nights of crying until you finally start thinking about something else
Besides the omnipresent question,
"Who will love me again?
Who will ever love me?"

      "For I'm not so old
      And I'm not so plain
      And I'm quite prepared
      To . . . "

Yes? What?

Look, it's like falling out of a twenty-story building.
All your good friends,
      they try to puff themselves up for you as soft as possible,
But they're still only couch pillows.
They may save your life when you hit them,
But you're still gonna break every bone in your body.

Feel sorry for yourself.
Sure, your tiny steel-ribbed mother told you never to do that,
But who the hell is going to do it for you?
"*Piangi, piangi,*" the old man in the opera tells Violetta.
"Cry, honey, cry." Do it right.
Do it yourself.

The sound of one hand clapping

LISE MENN

Snug with my coffee, winter morning, sunny window, comics,
On the verge of happy. Then the Question
Grins again its gut-ache: Am I being good?

                                        Good girl, bad girl;
Good wife, bad wife; good teacher, faithless friend —
At least I knew; could judge, defy, approve, or justify.
But now: Good widow? What the hell is that?
What balance struck between beloved shade and life?

Conundrum coiled in coffee cup:
          Am I doing this right? Should I do something else?
I can't be okay if I don't know if it's okay to be okay.

Without my other hand, how can I clap?

Tar

LISE MENN

You think you've stopped crying
And then the blues come back,
You wonder what brought them:
  The red pen?
  The wind in the yard?
  The plaid shirt in the bank?

   Your buried grief seeps to the surface,
Like oil under tar sands.

Let it go. It's the rich black residue of the past,
Dead life becomes this stuff that sticks to the soles of your feet,
Welling up when it damned well pleases.
Let it go.

Erv's Gift

AGNES G. HERMAN

Years ago, my beloved said to me, "I wish to 'go' first so that you can have some freedom! Suppose I go at 100, you take your time, at least until 102. That should give you a taste of freedom!" It was a grisly joke I rejected at the time.

In the end he had his way—he went first. He turned his head, he could not face goodbye, nor could I. He had given so much of his own true self to me. He shared small bits and pieces with the others. His gifts of caring and sharing he freely gave away.

Now that the storm of loss is quiet, I understand and cherish two special gifts he saved for me. Peacefulness was one, it surpassed all else, enabled me to face my widowhood with calm. Freedom was the other. His gifts have become promises kept. They are enormous, even as I miss him dreadfully.

Throughout our clergy years, he was the cynosure at parties, during meetings, in the living room. I was the proud wife, quiet and listening along with the others. In handing me the torch, he opened up cracks in the woodwork to which the dear people who loved him had relegated me.

Daily, I regret there is no magic with which to bring him back. He taught me, long ago, we have no sorcerer's sleeves, no power, just faith and our endless love. His calming words come back to me, the small phrase I remember most rings in my ears almost every day, "Let it go…!" When I harangued or agonized, he would plead, sometimes impatiently: "Let it go…!" Finally I understand that too, I must no longer anguish over the impossible. He lives in my heart, my memories, my dreams, but he is not in my reality.

From the beginning, I have asked myself and I continue to do so now, "what would Erv do…what would he expect of me?" I know him well—he never did lie down and sigh "woe is me." His spirit has helped me understand that he would not expect me to give in to my grief or give up on my growth.

My feet keep moving as my head and heart run to catch up. I do the things that I do and enjoy the people I wish to engage. I continue to be myself, as he would insist. I have discovered that I am doing exactly what I expect of myself. I share and exploit my talent. I enjoy support from others. I know what is good about me and what is not so good. Above all, I have no plans to give in or give up. He understands.

Of course there are moments when I wonder at my own tenacity, why go on alone. What is this gift of freedom he willed to me? Why do I keep on chasing deadlines, anguishing over language, trying new things, always saying yes, hardly ever no? Why do I endure the petty quarrels, conceits, and concerns of my children, my peers? Why do I still care?

I learned hard lessons of discipline and order from my parents, my teachers. I have absorbed to the fullest, the memories of love, caring, and faith that my sweetheart shared with me. Together, we prepared me for going down the road of loneliness in a state of calm and grace. I am a lucky widow! That is no oxymoron—it is a fact of my life. For 64 years I loved my man. I am a survivor of the war and peace of marriage, on my feet, happy, fulfilled, and victorious.

IV
A Different Life

Freedom

GILDA ZELIN

My daughter made an interesting comment while we were waiting for the Fourth of July parade to begin. She said I was a "free agent," meaning that I could come and go whenever I wanted to. That evening, I started to think about being a free agent, and how it really concerned me. I couldn't get the idea out of my head. Am I free—free from what?

Am I free to stay cozy in bed every morning and arise to start the day whenever I am ready? Then why do I have such restless nights and wake at the crack of dawn looking to snuggle, finding no one there, and rolling out of bed to start another long day?

Am I free from the responsibility of washing, cooking, shopping, and taking care of another person—in exchange for sitting around a lonely house, making plans a week in advance so that every day is occupied?

Am I free because I can do anything on a whim, anything I care to, without consulting the opinion of another person?

Am I free to hold the television clicker and change the station whenever I want? Then why, when it's not in use, do I hand it back to the blue chair?

Am I free to dress the way I want because you are not there to say, "How beautiful you are in my eyes"?

Am I free to put the heat up whenever I want and not worry that someone will turn it down? Then why have I suddenly become so conscious of conservation?

Are my clothes free as they cycle their way through the washer and dryer, no longer bothered by the extra-tall, large size clothing they had to tumble with? Do they feel free in a unisex environment?

Am I free, or has the rhythm of my life changed? My hours have changed in order to accommodate my friends, the single women and married women who have other responsibilities. In order to meet with anyone, I am using hours I never scheduled when my sweetie was alive. Does this make me freer, or am I just entering another life rhythm, and only *appear* to be a free agent?

Since your death, I have had to make many choices, cope with many problems. Notwithstanding all of this, my biggest effort will be to encompass the problem of how to change the rhythm of my life while still holding on to you, sweetie.

Am I free? *The only thing I am free from is you, my darling, and as a free agent I must learn to live with what it really means to be free…and alone.*

Repairs

JESSICA DE KONINCK

I almost went to visit the cemetery,
but you are not really there,
just what might be left
of the parts.   When you died
your brother refused to look
at the body.   *That's not Paul,*
anymore, he said.
                              I did look.
I sat and examined you closely,
a moment after you died, an hour
after, several hours after.
You would have done the same
for me, taking note of the details
of the flesh after life, what changed,
what remained the same.
Your hair still smelled like your hair
when the men came to remove
the body.   They would not let me
watch you go.

Instead of the cemetery I went
to Home Depot since it's on the same street,
but not as far away.   How funny
you would find me, navigating hardware,
electrical, plumbing supplies.
The whole place smells like men.
I miss that.
                    I walked past the yard bags
three times before I found them
and did not know to buy a switch
along with the light.   How you loved

meandering the overstocked
aisles, inspecting the intricacies
of toggle bolts, checking lumber for knots
and warping. It's my turn now.
I am becoming accomplished
in the small details of living alone.
I have learned to shim a table,
tighten a faucet, drill a hole.

The Walk Through

JESSICA DE KONINCK

After the movers left
our house spoke in voices

I had not heard before.
The storm door rattled.

Downstairs, a radiator clanged
awkwardly, like when you had hiccups,

and they would not stop.
That happens sometimes,

the doctor said.   What he meant was,
dying looks like this.

Morphine takes care of everything.
First, I threw out medications,

syringes, hospital bedding.
Then things got harder;

your clothes, your books, your tools.
The maple workbench went

to a woodshop in New York.
Architects bought your volumes on design.

But I could not find a home for your tuxedo.
Let's face it, I threw away

a lot. I'm not taking much
with me. I bought a new home.

It's very small.

Not Enough

P. C. MOOREHEAD

I wake up in the morning,
and I feel energetic.
When have I felt energetic?

Bounding from bed at first call,
shampooing my head so early—
something has changed.

This long night,
this passageway of grief,
has been run.

How grateful can I be?
Not enough.

Black Lace

BERNICE RENDRICK

Shadows fall on boards worn raw
contrast the sun-bleached deck
with filigree.

The bench my husband made
in a more energetic time
has held up well,
outlived him.

Old Douglas fir tree
reaches up beyond my sight—
deep crevices split bark
in the dark brown trunk
like aging skin.

Ruins Creek is dry
this third year of drought
but black lace
falls across the weathered deck
like a dropped shawl.

By the outside shower
green bamboo
catches a breeze
remembers to dance

Sixteenth Anniversary

TESS GALLAGHER

You died early and in summer.

Today, observing the anniversary
in a cabin at La Push,
I wandered down to the gray-shingled
schoolhouse at the edge of the sea.
A Quileute carver came out of a low shed.
He held classes in there, he said. Six
students at a time. He taught me
how to say "I'm going home"
in Quileute by holding my tongue in
one side of my cheek,
letting the sounds slur past it, air
from the far cheek
a kind of bellows.

I felt an entirely other
spirit enter my body.   It
made a shiver rise up in me
and I said so. The carver
nodded and smiled. He
said he taught carving
while speaking Quileute.
I imagined that affected
the outcome, for the syllables
compelled a breath in me
I'd never experienced before.

He showed me a rattle
in the shape of a killer whale
he'd been carving. The tail

had split off, but he said he
could glue it back. He let me
shake it while he sang
a rowing song they used
when whaling. My whole arm
disappeared into the song;
the small stones inside
the whale kept pelting
the universe, the sound
raying out into the past
and future at once,
never leaving the moment.

He told me his Quileute name,
which he said didn't mean
anything except those syllables.
Just a name. But I knew he
preferred it to any other. "I'm going
home," I said, the best I could
in his language, when
it was time to walk on
down the beach. Fog
was rolling in so the rocks
offshore began to look
conspiratorial. He offered
his hand to shake. Our
agreement, what was it?
Wordless. Like what
the fog says when it
swallows up an ocean.
He swallowed me up
and I swallowed him up.
And we felt good about it.

You died early and in summer.

Before heading to the cemetery
I made them leave the lid up
while I ran out to the garden
and picked one more bouquet

of sweet peas to fan onto your
chest, remembering how you
beamed when I placed them
on your writing desk in
the mornings. You'd draw
the scent in deeply,
then I'd kiss you on the brow,
go out, and quietly close
the door.

We survive on ritual, on
sweet peas in August, letting
the scent carry us, so at last the door
swings open and we're both
on the same side of it
for a while.

If you were here we'd
sit outside, accompanying
the roar of waves
as they mingle with the low notes
of the buoy bell's plaintive warning,
like some child blowing
against the cold edge of a metal pipe.
I'd tell you how the Quileute
were transformed from wolves
into people, though I'm unsure
if they liked the change.   I'm
not the same myself, since
their language came into me.
I see things differently.
With a wolf gazing out.
I can't help my changes anymore
than you could yours. Our life apart
has outstripped the mute kaleidoscope
of the hydrangea and its seven changes.
I'm looking for
the moon now. We'll have

something new
to say to each other.

August 2, 2004
for Raymond Carver
and for Chris Morgenroth, Quileute Nation

Is It Time to Cast Your Line?

CATHERINE TIDD

Dating becomes most widows' favorite subject with other widows, sooner or later. There's a good reason for that: we feel uncomfortable talking about it outside the fold. We're all in a different place when thinking about a new relationship. Some have moved forward. Some feel like they can't. And some "move forward" several times a week, thanks to Internet dating and quarter pitchers. Since you were committed before and didn't want to be alone then, there's a big chance you might not want to be alone now.

Don't you think dating is like standing on a ledge? You sweat, hoping that the bungee cord we call karma is going to hold. Some of us aren't afraid of heights and are ready to take the plunge. Some take one look at the view (which looks just fine without our innards splattered below, thank you very much) and step back. And some of us get as far as strapping on the bungee cord but ultimately need a push from a friend, whom we'll be mad at while we're swinging but whom we'll thank for the experience once we're standing on solid ground.

Many of us are afraid that once we put ourselves "out there," we may not like what we find. But let's think of it this way: If you've cast your line before when you met your significant other, what are the chances you caught the only good fish? Sometimes we come up with that smelly boot, but every once in awhile we hook onto a keeper.

I understand that if where we have been was hurtful, it's hard to imagine there could be anyone out there who might understand what we've been through. I'd like to try and put that notion into perspective. There is a pretty slim chance that you will catch someone who has led a perfect life. Chances are, they're scared of putting themselves out there too.

Over the years I've heard so many people say that what they had was perfect—that they lost their soul mates and will never find that again. I won't argue with that. If that's the kind of relationship you had, you're right. That's rare. But, it was rare before you found it. And still, you found it.

I have yet to meet one widow who hasn't changed in monumental ways as she has coped with her loss. Most of us have gotten to the point where we are not the "pleasers" we once were. We say what we think, we realize that life is precious, and we don't have time to be anything less than who we really are.

The truth is, I've changed so much that even if my husband met me now, I don't know if he'd even ask me out. I'm more independent. I'm more direct. And my sense of humor has taken a downward turn into the land of Sick and Wrong. So, if I'm different, why would I expect to find the same relationship? Why would I want the kind of man who was perfect for who I *was* but may not fit with who I am now? Shouldn't I hope to find someone who can appreciate the "new" me?

One final thought: If that person was your soul mate then, and now you're a different person, who's to say you won't find the soul mate for the person you've become?

Lunch Dates

MARCI MADARY

In my mary jane shoes and short, flared skirt,
     I feel darling today.

It is particularly on these days
          that I miss you standing behind me:

          your hands resting on the curve of my hips,
          kissing the side of my neck while
          peeking down the front of my sweater.

Asking if I have time for lunch.

The woman dressed in black is walking fast

KATHARYN HOWD MACHAN

toward a cafe on Duval Street where she
will order Cuban coffee in a mug
she'll grip with slender hands. She's forty-one.
So far her life has been the choice and bend
of marriage, two kids, house, the part-time job
where she feels she's invisible. But here
she knows she doesn't have to be the same
smooth person. No one cares if she buys lace
and leather, emeralds in a plastic bag.
It's almost midnight now and here she is,
her ears pierced twice, her hair a curling flame,
already on her tongue the sharp bright pull
toward dawn of *con leche* with sugar, all
her high-heeled sandals have to dance with now.

The Young Widow Revives

PHYLLIS WAX

The earth thaws,
sucks at my boots.
Sap's oozing.
The mild air fluffs my heart.

I find myself moving the ring
to my right hand,
eyeing male faces.

The indolence of winter
drops away. Birds gather twigs
and build, start over each day.
Buds loosen, dogs race
and play. I think I'll shave my legs.

Widow's Lament

VALERIE KOCKELMAN

"What do you want?" she asked,
when I told her I am lonely
now that my husband is dead.
"I'd like to be married again," I said.

I want someone to call me in the afternoon, around three, to say:
    "What's new, and
    How you doin', kid,
    Did you read the *Chronicle*
    and what the President said?
     And do you need me to pick something up?
    OK—some ice cream and bread."

In the afternoon, around three.

So, what do I want?
I want someone
    to tell me that what I said at that party was slightly imprudent,
    but, it hit the nail on the head, and what the hell...

Someone who is so wild about me that he declared
    I was the best-dressed woman there;
    didn't I think so, too?

Someone who respects me so much that he insists I tell him
    how to vote on those complicated California Propositions.
Someone to rub up against me, furtively,
    while we're standing in the kitchen,

Someone to grope in my direction
    as my back and cold feet touch his at bedtime.

Most of all,
I want my eyes to light up again,
   in the afternoon,
      when the phone rings,
         around three.

My Hierarchy of Needs

SUSAN MAHAN

Wanted: someone who already loves me.

48-year-old writer, widowed, seeks company.
Intelligent, curious, straightforward,
Capable of passion, but prone to bouts of grumpiness.
Self-absorbed men need not respond.

48-year-old widow,
out of step with the dating world,
seeks gentle-hearted partner for lessons.

40ish poetess seeks soulmate for a little free verse.

Extremely lonely 48-year-old woman
seeks two 25-year-old men
in the short run…
and one 50+ for the long haul.

Minimalist looking for man over 50 who can answer
the following question affirmatively:
Are you breathing?

Where Is Walter?

CARY FELLMAN

In October before he died, our daughter
walked the woodland paths with him.
They shuffled through fallen leaves
speaking little. Then he said,
    "I hope your mom finds someone
    to share her life. I think his name
    might be Walter."

I wonder where my Walter is. I hope
he likes to take early evening walks
and loves children, laughter,
good books and music.

I thought I'd met my Walter on a plane
to Miami but his wife was waiting there.
The next Walter was a boring man,
obsessed with health. He wore garlic.

Then I met Walter who played tuba
in the community band. He was
short and fat and chewed Tums.

Somewhere there may be a Walter
wondering when he will meet
a lady named Cary.

Lingering

MARY PACIFICO CURTIS

We're in the family room. It's a redwood, river rock mountain cabin feeling without a fire in the fireplace—the room where Doug and I spread ourselves on the big soft couch, draping limb over limb dropping into cushions, drifting into utter contentment together.

That is not what happens now. In this moment I decide that I need something from our bedroom and walk to the other end of our house. Opening the hall door, I hear a sound that I heard earlier in the day. I search the two bedrooms on either side of the hallway, inspect the closets and turn to our bedroom. I hear the sound again and turn back, this time noting a sheet draped over the glass shower door in the hallway bathroom.

"Who's there?"

The sheet moves in the way of someone trying to be still, not breathe. I pull the bathroom door shut and hold it tight.   I try to scream, but I hear only a gurgle before my throat closes. I try again, this time calling, "Doug…" My hoarse yell takes me from sleep to wakefulness, the sound building as I become alert.

Time is moving backwards. In the beginning it is today. I am a widow. It has been two years. I think, "I have so much more life to live." And then, to myself I know, "He's here with me."

Early on, probably in the first year after his death, I dream of a kiss. I'm kissing a man who does not look a bit like Doug. In my heart it is Doug. I call him Doug and he answers to that name, yet, to look at him, he is not Doug.

I start to go out with a widower whose wife died a year ago. We talk easily— he's a critic, I'm in PR. There's more than that, it's easy to talk. There's more than that, we touch. People who lose a beloved don't have the gift of intimacy. Every touch is a reminder. This man touches me and I hold his arm fondly as we cross the plaza to the theater.

I know he's not the one.

Pretty Soon, It Was

HEATHER CANDELS

One day you dropped dead
and pretty soon it was the next day
and I was shopping for coffins.

Pretty soon it was a week
and I threw away your toothbrush,
finished the last
of the cornflakes you started,
tossed the newspapers
you swore you'd read some day.

Then it was a month
and I gave away your shoes,
found myself a lawyer,
ordered official papers to prove
I was alone.

Pretty soon it was two months
and your autopsy report landed cold
in my mailbox smattered with words
that may as well have been hieroglyphics.

Later it was six months
and you weren't the only thing on my mind.

Another year
and the scent faded from your one shirt
I kept in the closet,
and then I looked at another man.

And suddenly there was another man
and another,
and none
of them were you.

Pretty soon it was ten years
and I tucked our wedding photo into a drawer.

It seemed like too many years when all
those babies who were born
the year you died grew up.

And when I almost forgot
the sound of your voice,
the brown of your eyes,
I donated your glasses to a worthy cause.

Pretty soon my hair was gray
and yours was still brown,
yet all of you was gone.

I Seek You in the Faces of Old Men

FLORENCE WEINBERGER

I seek you in the faces of old men,
shout into their ears, scale their craggy cheeks,
touch their bald spots, tough, often bumpy.
You would be that old, and I would never let you fall.
I might not have overlooked your frailties.
I might very well have grown impatient with your fumbling,
the inadvertent moan when you turned in bed.

These old men teach me who you might have become.
Some hold my elbow when we walk,
say I am still beautiful.
We gentle each other.
Slower to judge, we make slow love.
We don't give up easily.
I would love you better now than I did.

Fortune is severe and coy with us

JACQUELINE LAPIDUS

No desire in me before I saw you
scanning the horizon for your errant sailboat
unaccustomed boldness as the tide receded

suddenly aware of shoulders like bronze sculpture
conversation resonant in the lower register
turned my flushed face toward you my good ear

smile a flashing beacon in the twilight
stretched my tanned legs sucked in my stomach
feeling the pulse in my throat flutter

all my denial reduced to moisture
If today I do not touch your body
enclose myself tonight in a dark study

drift into sleep after solitary pleasure
imagining you hard and sweet against me

Author's Note:
The title of this poem and the lines in italics are from *The Book of the Hanging Gardens* by
the German lyric symbolist Stefan George (1868–1933). George's involvements were mostly
homoerotic, but these poems were written to a friend's wife.

The Widow Turns Down a Date

GAIL GILLILAND

My neighbor wants to fix me up
With his plumber friend, a Catholic
Who fathered five children
Then lost his wife.
I wasn't a good mother the first time around,
Am not Catholic, and even though
The plumber possesses a license,
Somewhere I was given a doctorate.

My neighbor sees a woman growing old alone
While I see a woman who no longer gives a damn,
Whose hair now tumbles gray and long
Heavy as iron on her shoulder bones
And who wears no make-up
And, if she puts on clothes
Puts back on in the morning
What she took off last night.

I don't need a plumber, so
Why does his plumber friend
Need a wife?

Widow's Car

PATRICIA WELLINGHAM-JONES

On the back seat
a basket large enough
to hold poetry books
and a bird-watcher's field guide
topped with a baseball cap
from the local museum,
a small towel for spills,
square box of tissues.

On the front seat—
in addition to driver—
her favorite perfume,
bottle of water from her well,
a map with directions
to the restaurant
where they'll meet
for their first date.

They Tell Me

CAROL TUFTS

Each grief bleeds out,
even the most anguished
sorrow must unwind
like a long hour striking
itself dumb. Time
fills the absolute
absence that is your death,
compels life to be taken up
like the forlorn border
of some outdated dress
refashioned to fit the new
lover who is kind,
but cannot hold
to kindness, whom words assure
I feel something. Nothing
to keep me, only this
busy ticking of the flesh
you quit too quick
when you groped free
from your own. Now I am
the ashes you were
seared down to and refined
of what I was, the renderings
perished colors I apply
to make it up. Tonight
they settle like a scrim
I recline behind,
the light gauzy
so he cannot see
who is there
gone missing.

Birthday

ELLEN STEINBAUM

And so I move another year away.
I have a new haircut now,
but you would recognize me still:
I look exactly
as if I were the same.

You will not grow old
or stooped or slowed.
Caught in crystal time
you wait
while I wear out,
while my body
imperceptibly accumulates
the weight of passing days
that we will spend apart.

I will be older than you
will ever be.
I will pass your age
become so old
that I am new,
and change a minute at a time
until nothing is left
of who you knew,

until the space between us lengthens
so that one day if you saw me
(if such a thing were possible)
you would mistake me
for a smiling distant relative,
an elderly aunt from crumbling photo albums.
You might sense a vague remembrance
and wonder if we'd ever met.

who would ask for this

ELLEN STEINBAUM

We are never so defenseless against suffering as when we love.
—FREUD

it is possible some say
to die of a broken heart
though I think too full
a heart can harm as well

> *why else this*
> *frazzledness tidy*
> *weft of days un-raveling in my hand*
> *favorite sauces curdled*
> *chicken roasting into*
> *dust while in his kitchen*
> *soufflés float on the ceiling*

rush of adrenaline stunning
muscle leaving it helpless un-
able to contract

> *my thriving houseplants drop their leaves*
> *wither curl refuse to*
> *bloom his finicky hibiscus*
> *grazes my head fourth*
> *generation mimosa*
> *shades me like Jonah's gourd*

prey to the danger of
expanding outward   out

but my heart beats
unbroken now no
recipe will save me
bright danger pleasure
poised for certain ambush
no safe place anymore

with no chance
of return

Last night his late wife

ELLEN STEINBAUM

came to him in a dream
then slid away, kept
slipping out of reach
down foreign streets
while I slept beside him
in our bed where my husband,
gone more than a decade now,
calls to me from time
to time, wants help
finding his cufflinks, keys.

A Hundred Forevers

ELLEN STEINBAUM

He's bought the wrong ones,
asked me to take them back
and so I slide the puny

roll of 42s—those
undistinguished flags—
across the counter, ask

can I exchange this and for
just two dollars more have
a hundred forevers.

Forever—not, we know, a word
to be believed: a note held on
past breath, the Dennis beach

beyond the oyster beds where
sand blurs into fog, or the
unlikeliness of this—our

stunned contentment that
has not, as yet, eroded into
boredom, irritation, those sodden,

all-too-human states that could
unspangle our small future.   But the
enormity turns doubt aside: in this quantity,

no option but belief.

Troubled in the Bedroom

LISE MENN

He spends the night here, Thursday.
I know you wanted this.   You told me, clearly.
And several times.   No conflict there.
                                    But this is still a widow's house,
Your pictures everywhere for me to look at; poems, tokens,
            little gifts between us.
I've left your bureau top just as it was; well, slightly neater,
Okay, and I did cash in that jar of pennies. But here's the fancy buckle
            from the belt
You finally and proudly wore the week before you died,
The candles that we liked to light, the incense burner. The statuette of Venus,
            and that fan.

What shall I do with you when he comes over?
Shove everything of you into the dresser drawer,
The one that holds one pair of undershorts, your favorite argyle socks, brown
            leather gloves,
Some incense sticks, your watch,
Your last new wallet, with your driver's license?

That pair of courting cranes: clearly a symbol, should I hide them?
And what about those candles? They won't pass for new.
No more will I—nor do I want to.

What can he bear of you? He knows that we were happy.
I have already watched my tongue these several weeks,
Not told him once how tall you were, nor how we sang together, long ago,
Nor any of a thousand other things, and never will.
If he's to be my lover, I can't let you haunt him.

I keep you for myself, for joy and sorrow. But where to put you, love?
Some secret altar? And shall I rescue you from drawers each time he leaves,
And stuff you in again when he comes over?

I will not be swept clean of you,
Nor will I hobble him.

Some answer must be found. And quick. It's Tuesday.

Beginning Again

LISE MENN

I. You will permit me, at times,
   To remember my dead husband,
And I will permit you to consider
   Your fleeting wives.

We will construct a new space
   For our minds to live
Stronger, at least in places,
   Because of what we have learned.

So I think we do well to remember
   Who is buried beneath the threshold,
For better or worse.

II. Six good-sized shelves of poetry—ten boxes at least
    Of books I hadn't yet got to reading
    Went off in a truck to California.

   I tried to make a list,
   Thinking maybe I would catch up, one by one,
   Taking them out of the library.

   Now you have come into my life
   With more poems than I will ever be able to read.
   Something balances here,
   Or not…

III. Beginning again is like:
     Putting on a back pack.
     Taking a back pack off.

Kissing again is like:
    Finding something thought totally lost.
    Finding something that never existed before,
    Except it was there all along.

  Fucking again is like discovering a new country
    Whose neighbors' customs and geography
    you think you might have studied.

  Beginning again is like understanding
    That I am not dead
    And neither are you.

IV. I can feel the hard places, the scarred places, the ice floes,
    Can try to poke carefully between them, looking for softness;

    Can issue maps, guidebooks, and bulletins
    With self-guided tours
    Of my own fault lines.
 Holding your hand before sleeping,
I find the word and the name I was wanting:
    Companion.

Each equal, each elder, each novice, by turns
Or all at once all of them,
We can keep company,
My dear, my companion.

V. Loving again is startling.
  I sputter for words like a hosed Cherubino
  But I know what it is,
    und darüber muss ich schweigen
  In thanks deeper and dumber than numb hands
    reaching toward a campfire,
  Feeling and remembering
  What it is to be warm.

Author's Notes

1. "...a hosed Cherubino / But I know what it is": *Voi, che sapete* (You who know): Cherubino's passionately confused canzone from the opera *Le nozze di Figaro*. Text by Lorenzo da Ponte (1749–1838), music by Wolfgang Amadeus Mozart (1756–1791).

> *Voi, che sapete che cosa e amor,*
> You, who know what love is
> *donne, vedete s'io l'ho nel cor!*
> ladies, see if I have it in my heart!

In traditional period costuming, Cherubino wears short trunks and hose; pun intended.

2. "...*und darüber muss ich schweigen*," after Wittgenstein, *Tractatus Logico-Philosophicus*, proposition 7: *Wovon man nicht sprechen kann, darüber muß man schweigen.* "What we cannot speak of we must pass over in silence." The Ogden translation renders it: "Whereof one cannot speak, thereof one must be silent."

This Morning

SUSAN CAROL HAUSER

This morning, with the loons calling across the lake, and a creature in the swamp galumping, and the drawl of a distant mourning dove pulling at me, so that I turn my head to listen better in one ear,

this late-July morning in northern Minnesota, with the leaves of the oak trees approaching their deepest green, and the reed canary grass outside my window already gone to seed, and the thistles that I let grow this year topping off with purple flowers, and the bay of the lake calm in the still air, the pelicans, in their morning cruise around the perimeter traveling each with its own image stitched alongside it, the image exactly equal to the pelican itself except that it does not exist,

this morning, this late-July morning, the trees speaking the tongue of songbirds, I do not miss you.

Message

JUDY BEBELAAR

I would like to put it on this paper for you
not on the paper really, but threaded through the words
words are our best inventions
metamorphosis, transcendence, transmigration
and yet I fall so short
can't seem to change, and into what?
certainly can't cross over
how can we meet?

you're on that side
I'm on this
and here I am with another
I almost called him by your name once

sometimes in dreams when you're coming home
I don't know what to do with the fact of his being here
in the dreams houses by water, wings,
boats that are beds

you rode waves as if you had wings
he makes houses into sailing ships
the kitchen a galley with high shelving
what used to be our bedroom
now a pilot house
where I write and look out
at the same trees you saw
in skies which still fold season into season
this is our home
yours, mine
now mine, his

the first time I said *love* to him
after the glider ride and my undeniable
greed for his kiss and more
he said *I don't know what love is*

I used to be so sure
should I have waited
until my ashes were taken to be scattered
with yours?
could we swim together then?

I think of running,
the simple intricate physics that moves me forward
the breath heart pumping transforming
body to spirit energy light
I don't know how
is that the secret to solving love?
just keep putting one foot in front of the other
and trust

when I think I've found the way
after a morning coupling that lifts the new two of us
into the blue of day
I remember the slow blessing of the Hopis,
their small rafts over silk water
making the ground sacred for movement
I think of how they had no word for past or present
how this is the fourth world, another chance to get it right
we live here and do our best

Einstein said that gravity cannot be held responsible
for people falling
in love
I chose to jump

from bright skies
I fall into memories of the hemlock you planned to take
when it was too painful, maybe too hopeless,
but you didn't, wanting to hold on
to me I suppose, and to our daughter,

and to the yellow primrose along the coast
trembling in the small breezes of evening,
to light glancing off ocean silver green
and to the light that explodes inside
when you're making love

and then those wings again
something about those wings and
falling through light
while feeling warm and climbing light again and soaring
down on Daedalus wings doomed
and still soaring and laughing
is what I wanted to try to tell you

Something

JUDY BEBELAAR

This has something to do with the *tap tap tap* of an early morning dream,
with traffic rushing by and people who talk too much
and jet exhaust and red-tailed hawks.
This has something to do with plum blossoms every February
And then hard rain.

This has something to do with the curve of future plans,
with Esalen, Constantinople, Positano, the French Riviera,
with trips that may never be made and hope gone awry.
This has something to do with fires, full lunar eclipses,
and sudden gusts of wind blowing down fifty-year-old elms.
This has something to do with nests falling out of trees.

This has something to do with swimming all the way to the raft,
and lying on hot wood with silty water drying on your skin,
a hand flung over your eyes to keep out the sun,
something to do with wars and babies,
with uterine cancer
and a nice calm game of draw poker.
This has something to do with birthdays
and friends, and just-missed trains,

something to do with cedar and spring bamboo,
with the shades of green and yellow in a sun-struck cornfield,
with the gaze directed at the horizon and balance.
This has something to do with moss between stones,
with blue between patches of clouds,
the moment between inhale and exhale,
with how John died that beautiful June,
and with how improbable it was that I met you
because of a broken hinge on a broken door

now the door to our bedroom
made lovely by your hands.

This has something to do with how I still miss him,
especially on June days when the sky is clear to the west,
with how wrong it was that he should die at only 49,
tall and strong and loving the ocean almost more than me.
And this has something to do with my love for you.

Epilogue

Widow and Dog

MAXINE KUMIN

In this last poem, a woman who is not widowed imagines what it might be
like to live alone and to attain a kind of serenity after the death of a husband
of many years.

—EDS.

After he died she started letting the dog
sleep on his side of the bed they had shared
for fifty-one years. A large discreet dog, he stayed
on his side but the tags on his collar jingled as he sighed
and especially when he scratched so she took his collar off
and then his smooth tawny bulk close to her but not
touching eased her through the next night and the next.

One morning, a chipmunk and his wife somehow slipped in
through the screen door when neither of them was looking.
She got up screaming from her coffee and whacked at them
with a broom. Dog pounced and pounced but they were faster
than he was and dove under the refrigerator. After a while
he stopped crashing into chairs and skidding around corners
in fruitless pursuit and then they came and went untroubled
even drinking out of his water dish, their tails at right angles.

That summer it just seemed simpler to leave the window
by the bird feeder open for ease of refilling. Some creatures
slipped casually out and in. The titmice were especially graceful.
She loved to watch them elevate and retract their crests
whenever they perched on the lips of the kitchen counter.
The goldfinches chittered and sang like drunken canaries
and once in a thunderstorm a barred owl blundered
into the fake crystal chandelier she had always detested.

Autumn fell on them in a joyous rush. The first
needles of hard frost, the newly sharp wind, the final
sweep and swirl of leaves, a swash of all-day rain
were not unwelcome. Hickory nuts ricocheted
off the barn's metal roof like a rain of BB gun pellets.
They both took afternoon naps. They both grew portly.
While Dog in his dumb allegiance dozed on the hearth,
sometimes he ran so fiercely in his dreams that he bared his teeth.
Reclusive comfortable Widow scribbled in her journal.
It did not matter how much she woolgathered, how late
into the night she read, it did not matter if she
completed this poem, or another.

Contributors

"ARIEL," a Pacific Northwest poet, describes being a widow as "an unnerving balancing act." Published in a variety of publications, including *AIM, Chemeketa Courier, Gold Man Review, Speaking Peace, Statesman Journal,* and *Unshod Quills,* and in literary anthologies, she actively participates in open mic and spoken word events in the Willamette Valley.

BARBARA BALD was a science educator for middle school students for 22 years. She also worked for NHPTV in instructional television, and as a counselor and teacher of life education. Presently she is a freelance writer and educational consultant. Her full-length collection of poetry is *Drive-Through Window.* Her recent chapbook is *Running on Empty.*

T. J. BANKS is the author of *A Time for Shadows, Catsong, Derv & Co., Souleiado,* and *Houdini,* a novel that the late writer and activist Cleveland Amory enthusiastically branded "a winner." *Catsong,* a collection of her best cat stories, was the winner of the 2007 Merial Human-Animal Bond Award.

MARILYN BATES, author of *It Could Drive You Crazy,* is a teacher-consultant at the National Writing Project at the University of Pittsburgh. She has read at the Library of Congress and the James Wright Poetry Festival. Her work has appeared in *The MacGuffin, The Paterson Literary Review, One Trick Pony, Poet Lore,* and *The Potomac.* Her one-act play *Life Without Nipples* was produced in 2007.

JUDY BEBELAAR is a retired San Francisco public high school teacher. Many of her poems are about her first husband John Bebelaar, who died of lymphoma at age 49. Alan Jencks, her second husband, continues to be understanding as well as proud and supportive of her work, which has been published widely.

MARIANNE BETTERLY writes poetry when she isn't hip-hop dancing, cooking quiches, or traveling to Kyoto. Her poems have been published widely in books and periodicals including the Hot Flashes series, *The Green Silk Journal,* and *The Haight Ashbury Literary Journal.* Marianne lives in Kensington, California.

ROSELEE BLOOSTON is an award-winning writer with plays produced nationally and internationally. Her publication credits include *AARP The Magazine.* Roselee founded Tunnel Vision Writers' Project and has taught in university programs. She is currently seeking representation for her novel, *Trial by Family,* and is writing a memoir, *Dying in Dubai.*

SUSANNE BRAHAM began taking undergraduate creative writing classes to help cope with the feelings unleashed by the sudden death in 2002 of her husband, a 56-year-old professor of medicine. Putting it in writing, giving it form, has been a great catharsis.

REGINA MURRAY BRAULT has twice been nominated for the Pushcart Prize. Her awards include 2007 Euphoria and SkySaje Enterprises International Poetry Competitions and the 2008 Creek Walker Prize. Regina's poetry has appeared in more than 130 publications. She leads The Cherry Lane Poets workshop in Burlington, Vermont.

HEATHER CANDELS, a Minnesota native, lives in Connecticut and teaches middle school English. She is a graduate of Manhattanville College's Master of Arts in Writing program. Her work has been published in *Inkwell, The Prairie Home Companion Newsletter, Heartlodge, The Rockhurst Review, Roux Magazine,* and *Xanadu,* among others.

ALISON KEELER CARRILLO keeps her husband's memory alive through a foundation in his name and a virtual museum commemorating his life and work: museoeduardocarrillo.org. His paintings and murals are as beloved as he was. Alison has fulfilled their family dream by adopting two sisters. She lives in the country near Santa Cruz with kids, animals, and a garden.

ANN CEFOLA is the author of *St. Agnes, Pink-Slipped* (2011), *Sugaring* (2007), and the translation *Hence this cradle* (2007). A Witter Bynner Poetry Translation Residency recipient, she also received the Robert Penn Warren Award judged by John Ashbery.

LENORE McCOMAS COBERLY, a native of West Virginia, lives and writes in Madison, Wisconsin. Her poetry, fiction, and essays have appeared in *The*

Christian Science Monitor, Wisconsin Academy Review, Sow's Ear, Nimrod, and other publications, and in two books from Ohio University Press. Her husband, an engineer, was steadfast in his respect for her writing. Her new book of poems is *For I am mountainborn.*

BARBARA J. COLLIGNON, married for almost 40 years, was present when her husband suffered a sudden fatal heart attack. She says: "My work as a translator and interpreter adds much joy to my life. My book clubs, choir, and circle of poet friends give me moral support. Family ties have grown stronger."

GAIL BRAUNE COMORAT, a founding member of Rehoboth Beach Writers' Guild, has been published in *Delmarva Review, The Broadkill Review, damselfly press, Delaware Beach Life, Gargoyle,* and *Apple Valley Review.* Widowed at 38, she's remarried and now resides in Lewes with her husband, Joe.

CHARLOTTE COX is currently writing poetry and fiction in Laconia, New Hampshire. Her poems have been published in the *Poets' Guide to New Hampshire* (2008 and 2010), *Poets' Touchstone,* and *The Poet's Place.* She has had articles published in *Library Journal, Public Libraries, New Hampshire To Do,* and *Seacoast Living.*

MARY PACIFICO CURTIS's poetry and prose have appeared in *LOST Magazine, The Rumpus,* Languageandcultures.net, Longstoryshort.us, *Clutching at Straws, Kaleidoscope* (Los Positas College Literary Anthology), *The Boston Literary Magazine,* and *The Crab Orchard Review.* When not writing, she is CEO of Pacifico Inc., a Silicon Valley public relations and branding firm.

JESSICA DE KONINCK's collection *Repairs* (2006) is a meditation on loss following the death of her husband, Paul. Her poems appear in a variety of journals, including the *Valparaiso Poetry Review, Paterson Literary Review, Lips,* and *The Ledge.* She has an M.F.A from Stonecoast and a B.A. from Brandeis.

PATRICIA FARGNOLI, New Hampshire Poet Laureate 2006–9, is the author of five books and two chapbooks. Her latest is *Winter.* Earlier books won the May Swenson Award and Jane Kenyon Literary Award. She has published in *Poetry, Ploughshares, Mid-American Review, Massachusetts Review* and many others.

SEREN FARGO has been writing poetry, primarily Japanese form, since 2007 and is founder/coordinator of the Bellingham Haiku Group. Her poems, published in the United States and internationally, have appeared in *Red Moon Anthology, Mu,* and *Yearning,* a memorial chapbook. She lives with her three cats in Bellingham, Washington.

ANNE CAIRNS FEDERLEIN served for nine years as a college president in Ohio and Kentucky. She was fired from the Ohio position when the chair of the board of trustees discovered her husband's illegal activities. Today, she is retired, lives in Chicago and writes about women's issues. Her favorite time is when she is with her three grandsons.

CARY FELLMAN has published six poetry chapbooks and is a member of Wisconsin Fellowship of Poets. Her work has appeared locally and nationally. She canes chairs, creates appliquéd quilts, and teaches Joy Through Movement® T'ai Chi Chih. Cary enjoys time with family and friends and admits an addiction to ice cream.

CONNIE FISHER began her career as a journalist in Mexico City and has continued as writer, journalist, and editor throughout the United States, including North Carolina where she resides today. She is the author of *Come Fly With Me,* a children's international adventure published in 2006, and coauthor of the autobiography of John Milano, *Doing It the Right Way* (2005).

MAUREEN TOLMAN FLANNERY's latest book is *Tunnel into Morning.* Others include *Destiny Whispers to the Beloved, Ancestors in the Landscape,* and *Secret of the Rising Up.* Her poems have appeared in 50 anthologies and over a hundred literary reviews. Maureen is a Wyoming native living in Chicago, where her four children were raised.

TESS GALLAGHER's nine poetry collections include *Midnight Lantern: New and Selected Poems, Dear Ghosts, Moon Crossing Bridge,* and *Amplitude.* She has also published three collections of short fiction, *Barnacle Soup: Stories from the West of Ireland* (with Josie Gray), essays, and a memoir about her late husband, Raymond Carver. She lives in Washington State and County Sligo, Ireland.

COOPER GALLEGOS was 30 when her poet-husband died, leaving her with two young sons. She says, "We moved to the open spaces of the Mojave Desert where the three of us healed and then thrived. I've published in anthologies and my novel *The Waterhauler* is now available."

ANDREA S. GEREIGHTY writes, "In 1974, I was attending college, raising my three children, and founded a public-opinion polls company that I am still active in today. I am the director of the New Orleans Poetry Forum. Many poems on the fascinating place I live, Louisiana, as well as others, have been published."

SANDRA M. GILBERT, Distinguished Professor *emerita* at University of California–Davis, has published eight poetry collections, including *Kissing the Bread: New and Selected Poems, Belongings* and *Aftermath*. Prose includes *Wrongful Death* (memoir), *Death's Door: Modern Dying and the Ways We Grieve; On Burning Ground* (essays), and *Rereading Women*, as well as *The Madwoman in the Attic, No Man's Land, The Norton Anthology of Literature by Women*, and other books coauthored or coedited with Susan Gubar.

GAIL GILLILAND's poems and stories have appeared in a number of journals. She's the author of a short story collection, *The Demon of Longing* (2002), and a poetics/memoir, *Being A Minor Writer* (1994). She lives in Massachusetts.

RUTH BADER GINSBURG has been an Associate Justice of the Supreme Court of the United States since 1993. In 1970, she cofounded *Women's Rights Law Reporter*, the first U.S. law journal that focuses exclusively on women's rights. Her late husband, Martin D. Ginsburg, taught tax law at Georgetown University.

PATRICIA L. GOODMAN, mother and grandmother, holds a degree in biology and spent her career breeding, training, and showing horses with her orthodontist husband. She now lives in Wilmington, Delaware, where she enjoys hiking, gardening, and photography, and has completed a book of poems, *Closer to the Ground*.

BARBARA L. GREENBERG is the author of several books of poetry—including *Late Life Happiness, The Never-Not Sonnets,* and *What Nell knows*—as well as *Fire Drills,* a collection of short fiction. She lives in Boston, Massachusetts.

FLORENCE GRENDE's stories and poems have appeared in *Babel Fruit, Poetica, The Sun, The Berkshire Review, The Women's Times,* HotMetalBridge.org, and in the anthology *Robot Hearts*. She holds an M.F.A. from the Stonecoast program at the University of Southern Maine. She is also the author of a memoir available for publication.

SUSAN CAROL HAUSER is a poet, essayist, and natural history writer. Her books include *Outside after Dark: New & Selected Poems, You Can Write a Memoir,* and *Wild Rice Cooking.* Her awards include a 2011 Minnesota State Arts Board Initiative Grant and a 2010 McKnight Artist Fellowship, Loft Award in Poetry. www.susancarolhauser.com.

JANE HAYMAN returned to writing in the current millennium. Past work appeared in *The New Yorker, The Nation* and many other journals, including *The Desert Review,* edited by her late husband. New poems have been published online, in recent issues of *Margie* and *Barrow Street,* and in her chapbook *Ghost Places* (2013).

AGNES G. HERMAN writes, "I am a retired social worker, an active writer. I married in 1945 and enjoyed 63 years of happiness. Our son's death as a result of AIDS in 1992 catapulted me into the AIDS awareness field. My writing has been published nationally. I write a weekly column for San Diego's *North County Times.* My daughter and grandson are living nearby."

DONNA HILBERT's books include *The Congress of Luminous Bodies* and *The Green Season*—both from Pearl Editions—and *Traveler in Paradise: New and Selected Poems* and *Transforming Matter.* She and her poetry appear in the documentary "Grief Becomes Me: A Love Story." www.donnahilbert.com.

JILL JACKSON was born in New Jersey. After earning a master's degree in theater, she moved to Israel in 1970. Seventeen years and two wars later, she settled in Maplewood, New Jersey, with her British-Israeli husband, Geoff, and their son, Ariel. Geoff died suddenly in 2009. Jackson writes: "I am an advocate for the disabled. Creative arts have sustained me."

MAREAN JORDAN taught writing and worked with teachers on adolescent literacy before moving from Berkeley, California, to central Oregon. She writes poetry and songs, finding inspiration in the Northwest's mountains, rivers, and high desert.

ROSALIND KALIDEN, widowed in 2004, holds a B.S., *summa cum laude* and M.Ed. from the University of Pittsburgh. She works as an English/speech teacher, reading specialist, voiceover talent, and TV commercial actor. She has work-shopped with Pittsburgh's Madwomen in the Attic and taken classes in memoir and playwriting. Her poetry has been published in *Taproot Literary Review* and *Compass Rose* and is to appear in *Voices from the Attic.*

VALERIE KOCKELMAN's husband of 36 years, father of their five children, died by suicide after 18 months of treatment, overdosing on the antidepressant a psychiatrist erroneously prescribed. After losing her malpractice lawsuit against the psychiatrist and medical clinic, she is writing a book about the experience, which will include the poetry she wrote as therapy.

JACQUELINE KUDLER lives in Sausalito, California, and teaches at the College of Marin in Kentfield. Her poems have appeared in numerous reviews, magazines, and anthologies. Her full-length collections are *Easing into Dark* (2012) and *Sacred Precinct* (2003).

MAXINE KUMIN's seventeenth poetry collection is *Where I Live: New & Selected Poems 1990–2010*. Her awards include the Pulitzer and Ruth Lilly Poetry Prizes, the Poets' Prize, and the Harvard Arts and Robert Frost Medals. She lives on a farm in central New Hampshire.

JACQUELINE LAPIDUS, a Boston-based editor, teacher, and translator, grew up in New York and lived abroad for more than 20 years—first in Greece, then in France where she was active in international feminist groups. Her poems have appeared in numerous periodicals and anthologies and in three collections: *Ready to Survive, Starting Over,* and *Ultimate Conspiracy.* Her Significant Other died suddenly in 2004.

IRIS LITT has two published poetry collections, *What I Wanted to Say* and *Word Love,* as well as poems in literary magazines, including *Onthebus* and *The Writer.* She has won awards for both poems and stories. Iris leads the Woodstock Writers Workshops and has taught at Bard College, SUNY/Ulster, Writers in the Mountains, and elsewhere.

BONNIE LOVELL is a writer, editor, and adjunct writing instructor at the University of North Texas from which she has degrees in English, history, and political science. She has also worked as a newspaper librarian and an oral historian. She lives in Denton, Texas.

"M" is an associate poetry editor for *Stirring: A Literary Collection,* administrator of an online poetry critique forum, and co-chair of the Oregon Poetry Association's Portland unit. Her chapbook *To That Mythic Country Called Closure* was published in 2013. She is allergic to any activity even remotely domestic (cooking, gardening, etc.), preferring instead to read.

KATHARYN HOWD MACHAN is professor of writing at Ithaca College and the author of 30 published collections of poetry, most recently *Belly Poems: Words of Dance*. Her poems have appeared in numerous magazines, anthologies, and textbooks, including *The Bedford Introduction to Literature* and *Sound and Sense*. She was Tompkins County's first Poet Laureate (2002), and she edited *Adrienne Rich: A Tribute Anthology*.

MARCI MADARY fell in love with poetry when she was a child and began writing poems during her teenage years. Marci currently works in the field of spirituality but continues reading and writing poetry, expressing who she is as a widow, mother of two, and daughter of the universe.

SUSAN MAHAN has been writing poetry since her husband died in 1997. She is a frequent reader at poetry venues and has written four chapbooks. Susan joined the editorial staff of *The South Boston Literary Gazette* in 2002. She has been published in a number of journals and anthologies.

LAURA MANUELIDIS, M.D., is a professor at Yale with scientific articles centered on chromosome organization and viral dementias. Nominated twice for a Pushcart Prize, her poems have appeared in *The Nation, Connecticut Review, Oxford Poetry, Innisfree Poetry Journal,* and *Evergreen Review.* She has a published book of poems, *Out of Order;* see also http://yalesurgery.org/neuropathology.

LUCIA MAY is a violinist who lives and teaches in St. Paul, Minnesota. Her poems have appeared or are forthcoming in *Main Channel Voices, Pemmican, Evening Street Review, Hot Metal Press, Burnt Bridge, Paperdarts, Talking Stick, Tall Grass,* the Prose-Poem Project, and *Little Red Tree International Poetry Prize Anthology*.

ANN MCGOVERN has embraced poetry after many years as a prize-winning author of more than 55 books for children, including *Stone Soup,* celebrating its 44th year in print. Her books are translated and published worldwide. McGovern's poetry has been published in over 60 literary journals and anthologies. Her latest book is *River of Glass*. www.annmcgovernpoet.com.

LISE MENN, coeditor of this anthology, is professor *emerita* of linguistics; she has two sons, a daughter-in-law, a stepdaughter, and four grandchildren. Earlier poems appeared in anthologies of poems by linguists. In 2007 she began writing about the loss of her husband, linguist William Bright, encouraged since 2008 by her new partner, poet and film historian Bruce F. Kawin.

JOAN MICHELSON's work has been featured in the British Council's annual anthologies of new writing from the UK. Her collection *Toward the Heliopause,* poems in conversation with her deceased husband's poems, was published in 2011. Originally from Boston, she lives in England and teaches at Birkbeck College, London.

P. C. MOOREHEAD moved to rural Wisconsin from California's Silicon Valley. She appreciates the beauty and quiet of the woods and the inspirational environment that they provide for her writing and reflection. Her poetry and prose have appeared in many anthologies and publications.

DIANA O'HEHIR is the author of six books of poetry and five novels and the recipient of several awards, including the Poetry Society of America's De Castellano Award and the Devins Award in Poetry. Her first novel, *I Wish This War Were Over,* was runner-up for the Pulitzer Prize. She taught at Mills College for 32 years, during which time she was chairperson of the Department of English and of the creative writing program.

MARY OLIVER has published many works of poetry and prose, including *Thirst* following the death of her partner of more than 40 years. Her most recent collection is *Dog Songs.* Her numerous awards include the Pulitzer Prize, the Shelley Memorial Award, a Guggenheim Fellowship, and the National Book Award. She lives in Florida and Provincetown, Massachusetts.

PAT PARNELL lost her husband Bill in January 2010, the month of their 62nd wedding anniversary. She keeps mentally and socially active with poetry and editing. Author of two published collections of poems, she writes a newspaper poetry column and serves as associate editor of *The Poets' Touchstone* and *Currents.* www.patparnell.com.

PAMELA MANCHÉ PEARCE's published work includes poems, essays, stories, and articles. She has also written a memoir, *Blue Crete: Four Summers of Love and Remembrance.* The founder of Poets Read Poetry (www.poetsreadpoetry. com) and former director of events and publicity for PEN, she lives, writes, makes art, and volunteers for hospice in Garrison, New York.

ELLEN PECKHAM is a poet and a visual artist. Her works combining both art forms and individual poems continue to be read, published, and exhibited across the United States and in Europe and Latin America. Three volumes of her haiga were exhibited in 2012.

BERNICE RENDRICK is a writer living in Scotts Valley, California. She received the In Celebration of the Muse Award for her chapbook *Trainsong*. Bernice is a member of Poetry Santa Cruz and in her eighties still enjoys every aspect of poetry.

ELIZABETH PAGE ROBERTS is an activist and poet living in Brooklyn, New York. Her work has appeared in anthologies (*We Have Not Been Moved, In the Spirit of We'Moon*), journals including *The Isis Papers, Erasure,* and *Liquid Sky,* and numerous *We'Moon* calendars. With two other experimental poets, she also wrote *Cantle, Rubus and Oarlock*. After years at the War Resisters League, she is pursuing an M.F.A. in creative writing at Brooklyn College.

RUTH S. ROTHSTEIN lives in Boston and works as an editor in educational publishing. She hopes that jazz lovers will continue to listen to the music of her late husband, Jacques Chanier.

HELEN RUGGIERI lives in Olean, New York. She has two new books, *Butterflies Under a Japanese Moon* and *The Kingdom Where Everybody Sings Off Key*. Other poems have appeared recently in *Paterson Literary Review, Blue Collar Review, Adanna,* and *Earth's Daughters*. Visit http://www.helenruggieri.com/

NATASHA SAJÉ is the author of three books of poems, *Red Under the Skin* (1994), *Bend* (2004), and *Vivarium* (forthcoming 2014), plus many essays. She is a professor of English at Westminster College in Salt Lake City and has been teaching in the Vermont College M.F.A. in Writing program since 1996.

PATRICIA SAVAGE is a widow, a poet, and an educator. She runs a program for differently abled teens called Community Based Instruction that helps them start interesting lives after high school. She has yet to find anything more interesting than ordinary life or as challenging as the white page.

REBECCA SCHENCK lives in Charlotte, North Carolina, in a house she and her husband built over 40 years ago. A graduate of Salem Academy, Queens College, and University of North Carolina–Charlotte, she taught at both colleges, stopping to work and travel with Gordon, an architectural photographer. Rebecca, a former president of Charlotte Writers Club, has published poems and nonfiction.

JOANNE SELTZER's poems have appeared in many literary journals and anthologies. Her most recent poetry collection is *Women Born During Tornadoes.*

Joanne's poem "I Sing the Shekhinah's Praise" was chosen as a runner-up in the most recent Charlotte Newberger Poetry Competition and was published in *Lilith,* a Jewish feminist magazine.

KRISTINE SHOREY has been writing for a decade, after spending 15 years working for large corporations. She began writing to help process her experience of being widowed at age 29. Her 33-year-old husband was diagnosed with a brain tumor only 18 months after their wedding.

CHRISTINE SILVERSTEIN has relocated to Magnolia, Massachusetts, from Nantucket Island where she lived for 22 years, seven as a newlywed and 15 as a widow. The year her police sergeant husband died, she founded Sustainable Nantucket, a nonprofit organization cultivating the island's economy while protecting its character. She writes journals and short essays to help weave her grief through her joy for life.

ANN SINCLAIR is a poet and clinical social worker who lives in Portland, Oregon. Her work has appeared in *Verseweavers* and *The Oregonian.*

ALINE SOULES's work has appeared in numerous journals and anthologies. Poems from *Evening Sun: A Widow's Journey* have appeared in *Kaleidowhirl, Reed, Shaking Like a Mountain,* and *Houston Literary Review.* Prose poems from *Meditation on Woman* (2011) have appeared in *Tattoo Highway, Poetry Midwest, Newport Review,* and *Kenyon Review.*

ELLEN STEINBAUM is the author of three poetry collections: *Brightness Falls, Afterwords,* and *Container Gardening;* and a play, *CenterPiece.* Her work has been nominated for a Pushcart Prize and included in Garrison Keillor's *Good Poems, American Places.* A former columnist for the *Boston Globe,* she blogs on "Reading and Writing and the Occasional Recipe" at www.ellensteinbaum.com.

CAROLYN STEPHENS was born in 1961 and widowed in 2009. Mother of a daughter in college, she writes about grief, healing, and The New Normal ("whatever that is"), in her blog throughawidowseyes.wordpress.com. She says, "The online grief community has been a great source of comfort and connection. I am honored to be part of this anthology."

CHRISTINE THIELE writes for several grief publications and websites and is a contributing author and blogger. Her "Memoirs from Widow Island: A Journey

Toward Healing" can be found at www.widowisland.wordpress.com. Her husband's death in 2005, her grief journey, her hope of survival and healing, and her family inspire her writing.

CATHERINE TIDD is the founder of www.theWiddahood.com and author of a memoir, *Confessions of a Mediocre Widow.* She has contributed to several anthologies on grief and renewal and, as a motivational speaker, focuses on finding joy after loss. Catherine is also a speaker for the Donor Alliance of Colorado.

TAMMI J. TRUAX was widowed at 38. Among the many tumultuous changes that brought to her life was a career change to writing. She works freelance from home, while raising two children, as a newspaper columnist and radio show producer; and she has just finished her first novel. Tammi is also co-founder of The Prickly Pear Poetry Project, a workshop for people affected by cancer. She blogs at www.aintiawriter.blogspot.com.

CAROL TUFTS teaches drama in the English Department of Oberlin College. Her poems have appeared in a number of literary magazines, including *Poetry, Poet Lore, Poetica,* and *Iconoclast.* She is a recipient of an individual artist award from the Ohio Arts Council and is at work on a collection of poems.

ELIZABETH VON TRANSEHE is a high school French teacher in the San Francisco Bay Area. She lives with her second husband, daughter Zoe, and baby son William.

DONNA WAIDTLOW lived in the Alaskan wilderness as a young woman and started her family there. When she returned to civilization, she found her way to poetry. Donna earned her M.F.A. from Goddard College. She received the Floating Bridge Press Chapbook Award in 1997 for *A Woman Named Wife.*

PHYLLIS WAX, a Pushcart-nominated poet, lives and writes on a bluff overlooking Lake Michigan in Milwaukee, Wisconsin. Her work has appeared in both online and print publications, including *Out of Line, Your Daily Poem, Verse Wisconsin, Seeding the Snow,* and *Ars Medica.* She co-edited the 2002 Wisconsin Poets' Calendar.

FLORENCE WEINBERGER is the author of four collections of poetry, *The Invisible Telling Its Shape, Breathing Like a Jew, Carnal Fragrance,* and *Sacred Graffiti.* Twice nominated for a Pushcart Prize, her poetry has appeared in numerous literary magazines and anthologies, including *Poetry East, Comstock Review, Antietam Review, Rattle, Nimrod,* and *Calyx.*

PATRICIA WELLINGHAM-JONES is a former psychology researcher and writer/editor with an interest in healing writing and the benefits of writing and reading work together. Widely published, she writes for the review department of *Recovering the Self: A Journal of Hope and Healing* and has ten chapbooks of poetry.

KATHERINE J. WILLIAMS, associate professor *emerita* at George Washington University, works as an art therapist and clinical psychologist. Her articles have appeared in *The American Journal of Art Therapy* and *Art Therapy.* She has poems in journals such as *The Northern Virginia Review, Poet Lore,* and *Entelechy International,* and in *The Poet's Cookbook* and *Portrait of the Artist as Poet.*

NANCY H. WOMACK, a retired community college educator, holds a Ph.D. in modern British literature from the University of South Carolina. In 2005 she lost her husband of 42 years to cancer. Writing about his illness and death helped her regain her own sense of identity in a dramatically different environment.

HOLLY ZEEB is a psychologist in the Boston area who gardens, cycles, and spends time with family in Maine. Through poetry she is able to see more clearly, to protest, to preserve, and to let go. Her poems have appeared in numerous journals and anthologies and in a chapbook, *White Sky Raining.*

GILDA ZELIN, born in Brooklyn, New York, is a former teacher and published author. She now lives in Santa Cruz, California. Her latest passions are Progressive Painting for her soul and quinoa for her body. Her days are spent writing, walking, and practicing yoga.

THELMA ZIRKELBACH is a speech pathologist during the day and a writer at night. She has published romance novels, essays, and several poems. Thelma blogs at www.widowsphere.blogspot.com. Her memoir, *Stumbling Through the Dark,* was released in February 2013.

Permissions and Acknowledgments

Tess Gallagher, "Paradise," "Wake," "Deaf Poem," "Crazy Menu," "Ring," "Dream Doughnuts," and "Sixteenth Anniversary" from *Midnight Lantern: New and Selected Poems.* Copyright © 1992, 2006 by Tess Gallagher. "Crazy Menu" and "Ring" from *Moon Crossing Bridge.* Copyright © 1992 by Tess Gallagher. All reprinted with the permission of The Permissions Company, Inc. on behalf of Graywolf Press, Minneapolis, Minnesota, www.graywolfpress.org.

Sandra M. Gilbert, "Berkeley: Anniversary Waltz Again," "October 29, 1991, 4PM, Outside Saratoga Springs," and "November 26, 1992: Thanksgiving at Sea Ranch, Contemplating Metempsychosis," from *Ghost Volcano: Poems* by Sandra M. Gilbert. Copyright © 1995 by Sandra M. Gilbert. Used by permission of W. W. Norton & Company, Inc.

Maxine Kumin, "Cross-Country Lines," from *Ghost Places* by Jane Hayman. Used by permission of Finishing Line Press.

Mary Oliver, "Widow and Dog," from *Jack and Other New Poems* by Maxine Kumin. Copyright © 2005 by Maxine Kumin. Used by permission of W. W. Norton & Company, Inc.

"After Her Death" and "Those Days," from *Thirst* by Mary Oliver—Published by Beacon Press Boston. Copyright © 2006 by Mary Oliver. Reprinted by permission of The Charlotte Sheedy Literary Agency Inc.

Grateful acknowledgment is made to the following authors for permission to reprint their previously published work in this anthology:

Barbara Bald: "Snapshot" and "Ghost of Prescott Park" in *Drive-Through Window: Poems* (Walch Printing 2012).

Judy Bebelaar: "Message" in *Willard & Maple: Literary and Fine Art Magazine of Champlain College*, vol. XIII (2008) and *Flyway: A Journal of Writing and Environment* 12:2 (Iowa State University 2009); "Something" in *Schuylkill Valley Journal of the Arts* 26 (Spring 2008).

Heather Candels: "Pretty Soon, It Was" in *Xanadu 2009* (Long Island Poetry Collective).

Ann Cefola: "What Yields to Winter" in *Sugaring* (Dancing Girl Press 2007).

Jessica de Koninck: "Salvage," "Pillow Talk," "The Golem," "Repairs," "I Want to Ask You," and "The Walk Through" in *Repairs* (Finishing Line Press 2006).

Patricia Fargnoli: "Old Woman Dreams" in *Duties of the Spirit* (Tupelo Press 2005) and *Love Over 60* (Mayapple Press 2010). Reprinted by permission of the author and Tupelo Press.

Seren Fargo: "Guilt," "don't," "spring cleaning," and "death anniversary" in *Yearning* (Leaving Tracks Publishing 2011); "Unpalatable" in *Whatcom Hospice Bereavement Newsletter* (Winter 2009) and *Yearning* (Leaving Tracks 2011).

Cary Fellman: "If I Write Enough" in *Remembering* (Gladly Press 2006).

Maureen Tolman Flannery: "Falling" in *KARAMU* 18:2 (Spring 2003) and "The Farmer's Widow Gives Him a Piece of Her Mind" in *Pudding* (2002).

Barbara L. Greenberg: "The Widow of Few Tears" in *Late Life Happiness* (Parallel Press 2010).

Jane Hayman: "Cross Country Lines" in *Ghost Places* (Finishing Line 2013).

Donna Hilbert: "Deshacer" in *The Congress of Luminous Bodies* (Aortic Books 2013).

Maxine Kumin: "Widow and Dog" in *Love Over 60: An Anthology of Poems* (Mayapple Press 2010).

Jacqueline Lapidus: "Fortune is severe and coy with us" in *Origami Condom* #12 (Oct. 2008) and "With friends like these . . ." in *Marco Polo* (Jan. 2012. www.marco poloartsmag.com).

Iris Litt: "Death of a Friend" in *Onthebus* #13 (1993) and "Grief" in *Stonemarrow* (defunct)

"M": "Shoes brought me to this place" and "When one door closes" in *Half-Drunk Muse* (Spring 2006), "Salt" in *Rattle* #32 (Winter 2009), and "Fresco alfresco" in *Prick of the Spindle* 2:3 (Sept. 2008); "When one door closes," "Shoes brought me to this place," "Salt," and "To a husband, saved by death," in *To That Mythic Country Called Closure* (2013).

Laura Manuelidis: "Phantom Limb," "Chora," and "Until" in *Out of Order* (iUniverse 2007).

Diana O'Hehir: "Thirty Years" in *Field* (Spring 2011), "Boats," and "Why Can't I Dream About Him?" in *Poet Lore* 106:1/2 (Spring/Summer 2011).

Ellen Peckham: "323 West 22nd Street" in *Penumbra* (2011).

Natasha Sajé: "Circumflex" in *Literary Imagination* 14:1 (2012).

Patricia Savage: "How Could I?" in *The Poets Touchstone* (Poetry Society of New Hampshire 2011).

Aline Soules: "Apart" in *The Houston Literary Review* (May 2009), *Qarttsiluni* (Aug. 2010), and *On Our Own: Widowhood for Smarties* (Abilene, TX: Silver Boomer Books 2012).

Ellen Steinbaum: "Birthday" in *Afterwords* (Blue Unicorn 2001), "Last night, his late wife" in *Innisfree Poetry Journal* (Spring, 2011) and *Brightness Falls* (CW Books 2013); "who would ask for this" and "A Hundred Forevers" in *Brightness Falls* (CW Books 2013).

Christine Thiele: "Surviving with Gratitude" and "Persevere and Endure" in *Memoirs from Widow Island* (Apr. 27, 2010 and Oct. 23, 2009, widowisland.wordpress.com).

Catherine Tidd: "Is It Time to Cast Your Line?" in *Widdahood Post* (June 30, 2010, www.thewiddahood.com).

Florence Weinberger: "I Seek You in the Faces of Old Men" in *Love Over 60* (Mayapple Press 2010).